ROUTLEDGE LIBRARY EDITIONS:
THE LABOUR MOVEMENT

Volume 34

PROTEST OR POWER?

PROTEST OR POWER?

A Study of the Labour Party

MARGARET STEWART

Routledge
Taylor & Francis Group

LONDON AND NEW YORK

First published in 1974 by George Allen & Unwin Ltd

This edition first published in 2019
by Routledge
2 Park Square, Milton Park, Abingdon, Oxon OX14 4RN

and by Routledge
711 Third Avenue, New York, NY 10017

Routledge is an imprint of the Taylor & Francis Group, an informa business

British Library Cataloguing in Publication Data
A catalogue record for this book is available from the British Library

ISBN: 978-1-138-32435-0 (Set)
ISBN: 978-0-429-43443-3 (Set) (ebk)
ISBN: 978-1-138-32552-4 (Volume 34) (hbk)
ISBN: 978-1-138-32555-5 (Volume 34) (pbk)
ISBN: 978-0-429-45035-8 (Volume 34) (ebk)

Publisher's Note
The publisher has gone to great lengths to ensure the quality of this reprint but points out that some imperfections in the original copies may be apparent.

Disclaimer
The publisher has made every effort to trace copyright holders and would welcome correspondence from those they have been unable to trace.

Protest or Power?

A Study of the Labour Party

MARGARET STEWART

London · George Allen & Unwin Ltd

Ruskin House · Museum Street

First published in 1974

© George Allen & Unwin Ltd 1974

ISBN 0 04 351048 5 hardback
     0 04 351049 3 paperback

Printed in Great Britain
in 11 point Times Roman type
by Willmer Brothers Limited, Birkenhead

CONTENTS

INTRODUCTION

'Bevanites rebuffed by Margaret Stewart' proclaimed a *News Chronicle* placard outside the Grand Hotel, Scarborough. 'I didn't know we had even propositioned her,' was the caustic comment of Dick Crossman, as he made his way to the Spa Grand Hall where the Labour Party conference was being held.

I don't remember the precise issue, but it was in 1954, at the height of the bitter conflict between the right and the left. During the years when the party was busy tearing itself to bits I had a ringside seat at the press table and lived through all the agonies and anguishes of the Bevanite crisis. After my paper collapsed in 1960 I followed the fortunes of the party more remotely, and perhaps more objectively, though in 1964 and 1966, as a Labour candidate for Petersfield, I joined battle with the squires and retired Admirals who assured the Tory candidate a sweeping victory in this rural corner of Hampshire.

To write a book about the Labour Party in the 1970s may seem the height of temerity, when so many books, articles and pamphlets have already been written and will go on being written.

The reader who looks for scandal and gossip will be disappointed. There are no inside revelations, no stories about what *X* said to *Y* over dinner at St Ermin's or over fish and chips at the ABC. This book is intended to help the not so sophisticated reader who is interested in politics but cannot afford the time or the money to study the more expensive volumes that have appeared about the Labour movement or the ever-increasing flow of politicians' memoirs. It is an attempt to draw together some of the threads and to describe some past events and present trends, as well as a few of the leading personalities. The pattern is episodic and by subject-matter rather than chronological. Historical references are used when they seem necessary to an understanding of current developments, for example the deep scars left by the MacDonald 'betrayal' of 1931, or where they are relevant to present policies.

Bill Simpson in his admirable study of the party and the unions[1] wrote that to write about the Labour movement was 'like trying to empty Loch Lomond with a teaspoon'. For my part I feel rather like Dame Partington, trundling her mop and trying to push back the Atlantic Ocean. So many new aspects keep emerging, so many events sweep in with the ceaseless tide, that it becomes an unequal contest with time and with the vastness of the problem.

I realise that there are many gaps in this book, but I have exercised the discipline of setting limits, in the hope that it will at least stimulate interest and provide a guide to further reading.

Within these limits, the main aspects covered include the record of the Wilson Governments, the party machinery and processes and Labour's relations with the unions. It looks at Labour leaders, past and present, the controversy over Europe, the relations between conference, the National Executive Committee and the Parliamentary party, and the way policies are made.

When I first thought of writing about the Labour Party, in the spring of 1972, the future looked very bleak. So much so, that I thought of calling it 'The crumbling coalition' or even 'The strange death of Labour England'. It seemed that social democracy had failed and that the divisions within the party, particularly over Europe, would result in permanent and unhealable fissures. But, after much research and talking to people at all levels, I was struck by the sense of continuity in the movement, by its resilience and apparent ability to discard its centrifugal tendencies at the approach of an election. And so a rather different, and more hopeful, picture began to emerge which could yet defy the critics and sceptics who have so often written off the Labour Party's chances.

The trouble about writing about contemporary events is to know when to stop. I had originally decided on March 1973. At this time there were signs that the party was pick-

[1] Bill Simpson, *Labour, the Unions and the Party* (Allen and Unwin 1973).

ing up momentum and regaining its morale – despite the by-election results and, in particular, the bitterness over Dick Taverne's victory at Lincoln.

In the end I was able to add a final postscript. This brings the story to the end of October 1973 and looks at the Blackpool conference, when the whole movement embarked on a leftward course, and peace, or at any rate a cease-fire, was declared between the various elements of the coalition.

My thanks are due to many friends in the party, the unions and Fleet Street, who have helped me with advice and information. I am particularly grateful to Terry Pitt, the party's research secretary, for information about 'Participation '72' and to Mrs Wagner, the party's Librarian. But the responsibility for everything in the book is entirely my own.

I

After June 1970

Summing up Labour's post-election conference in 1970, Ian Mikardo, the party chairman, said: 'If I can detect a single dominant theme running through the proceedings of our conference . . . it seems to be the argument about whether we are a party of power or merely a party of protest.' He went on: 'We Socialists do not seek power for its own sake. . . . Power is not an alternative to protest, it is complementary to protest. Indeed, it is the instrument through which protest issues in action.' We Socialists protest against the injustice, the ugliness, the inefficiency and the inhumanity of the selfishly acquisitive society and we seek power precisely to remedy those evils.

Mikardo, of course, was perfectly right. No political party could survive if it were solely interested in protesting. It must be motivated by the desire to gain and retain power, carrying as many voters as possible with it.

Douglas Houghton, the chairman of the Parliamentary Labour Party, who represents the moderate wing of the party as distinct from Mikardo's ultra-leftism, put it another way: 'The whole purpose of politics is power. Political parties are out to win power. Opposition parties strive and campaign for office. To become the Government is what this is about.'[1]

The history of the Labour Party down the years suggests that theory and practice do not always coincide. The party was brought into being because neither of the two established political parties, alternating between Government and Opposition with the inevitability of the couple in the barometer, could satisfy the aspirations of the organised workers. But to have a voice and a vehicle of expression

[1] *Political Quarterly*, October-December 1972.

was a different matter from striving to become the government. The early Labour leaders were interested only in protest and in representation. Labour had to wait for over twenty years before it could even approach the corridors of power.

There have been six Labour Governments in this century (excluding the Coalition under Churchill): 1924, 1929–31 under Ramsay MacDonald; 1945–50, 1950–1 under Attlee and 1964–6, 1966–70 under Harold Wilson. In none of these periods of office, with the possible exception of the early years of the Attlee administration, did the Labour Party come within measurable distance of achieving the objectives for which it stood.

The firm foundations of the welfare state and the National Health Service were laid before 1947 and key industries like coal and the railways were taken into public ownership. Thereafter, as R. H. S. Crossman has commented, the Attlee Government 'ran out of steam and almost disintegrated in power'. In 1924 Labour was a minority Government and in 1950 its majority was so slender as to inhibit any attempts at fundamental change even if there had been any desire for it. The 1929 MacDonald Government collapsed in the face of the world economic crisis. In 1966 the Wilson Government was 'blown off course' by shattering economic and financial events which it was powerless to control. Wilson battled on, but pursued deflationary policies which meant the shelving, if not the abandonment, of many of its long-term plans for social progress. It was beginning to recover its momentum in the last few months of its lifetime and Wilson had no reason to doubt that he would not be re-elected for a third term as Prime Minister. This was the message of all the opinion polls in the summer of 1970.

Labour clearly underestimated the extent to which the political pendulum was likely to swing. The British electorate traditionally likes to see a change of government after a reasonable period.

Even though voters have been more volatile in the twentieth century than they were in the days when Gladstone and Disraeli regularly changed places, there is still a tendency to let the Opposition party have its turn. It was disillusionment with the Liberal Coalition after the First World War that first brought Labour to office, and the long period of Conservative rule after 1931 produced a tremendous reaction in favour of Labour in 1945. The pendulum refused to swing in 1959, but in 1964 the campaign was dominated by the feeling that it was 'time for a change'. The Labour Party which skilfully exploited this feeling seemed to offer an exciting alternative to the tired and discredited Tories. In 1966 there was a general disposition to let the Government carry on what it had begun. Opinion polls show that the public tends to identify Labour as the party best equipped to deal with social reform, while the Tories are regarded as better managers. The 1966 slogan 'You *know* Labour Government works' was designed to show that Labour was efficient, as well as compassionate.

Every Labour Government, when it comes to office, is convinced that it is there 'for keeps' and that social democracy is in some way the natural Government for the British people, with their highly developed sense of fair play and tolerance. If Sweden can have a social-democratic government for forty years, why shouldn't Britain, the argument runs. In practice the analogy with Sweden cannot be carried too far, in view of the wide differences in size, population, traditions and temperaments. But Sweden, with its egalitarian philosophy and reformist trends, has continued to provide a beacon for British socialists.

Certainly the back-bench MPs who sang the Red Flag in the House of Commons in 1945 believed that a new and lasting political era had been ushered in. They cheered enthusiastically when Hartley Shawcross declared: 'We are the Masters not only for now, but for a long time to come.' I remember Ernie Bevin, in contemplative mood over a glass of Scotch in the Strangers' bar in the House saying in 1950: 'We'll get back. They like us don't they? Why should they want to turn us out?'

Such was the sense of confidence in the long-term future that a Fabian meeting was held at Buscot Park in the late

1940s entitled 'Labour – the next 15 years'. Hugh Gaitskell was one of the main participants.

Later, the aim of Harold Wilson, who became the first Prime Minister to lead his party to power with an increased majority in a second election (and narrowly missed winning a third term) aimed to make Labour the 'natural' Government of Britain.

Having at last achieved a surplus in the balance of payments and with his own personal standing high, he felt confident of a future in which he could consolidate Labour's position and push through some of the more fundamental measures urged upon him by an impatient party. 'Now Britain's strong, let's make it great to live in,' was the theme of a somewhat hastily concocted election manifesto in the summer of 1970.

But the 'fickle' electorate thought otherwise. People were fed up with rising prices and strikes, and were attracted by the Heath promises – so soon and callously to be broken – to curb price rises 'at one stroke' and deal with the trade unions.

Back in Opposition, it took an unconscionable time for Labour to lick its wounds and regain its self-confidence. Indeed, in some ways, the party gives the impression that it is more comfortable in Opposition than in Government. When it has a tiny majority, as in 1964, members are subject to a strict self-imposed discipline and few want to be accused of 'rocking the boat'. In Opposition Members can protest about mean and inadequate Tory policies, indulge in semantic arguments about socialism and draw up blue-prints for the future without too much thought for their costs or practical realities.

They do not need to compromise in order to keep 'their' Government in office.

Frank Cousins typified this attitude when he told a union conference in March 1960 (at the height of the conflict with Gaitskell over Clause Four): 'We are not going to run away from our principles in order to get votes.' Later, he said: 'We have never thought that the most important job the politicians do is to return themselves to the House of Commons.' Much the same thoughts were expressed by

Nye Bevan, ten years earlier, when he said: 'I am not interested in the election of another Labour Government. I am interested in the election of a Government that will make Britain a socialist country.'

Such views may be those of a minority within the party, but they reflect a stream of opinion which has to be reckoned with.

At such times one can detect a martyrdom complex, if not an actual death-wish. Donald Chapman, a former Labour MP in a penetrating article in the *Guardian* (8 November 1972) wrote: 'There are occasions during office when Labour seems to have the death-wish . . . In the same way there is a thankful rush back to protest when power is lost.'

The Conservative Government lost no time in demolishing the policies and dismantling the institutions set up by the Labour Government. The Prices and Incomes Board, the Consumer Council, the Industrial Reorganisation Corporation, the Land Commission and the Ministry of Technology were all among the casualties. Decisions were taken to hive off the profitable sections of the nationalised industries, to bring in commercial broadcasting, impose cuts in public spending and extend the principle of selectivity – a euphemism for the 'means test' – in the social services. The unemployment figure continued to creep up and by the winter of 1972 had reached the one million mark, the highest post-war figure on record. Despite the Chancellor of the Exchequer's proposals to stimulate the economy, business was slow to react and there was a falling off in investment. Prices continued to rise, particularly food prices, while rents were expected to increase rapidly as a result of the Housing Finance Act. Under the Labour Government, just over 24 million working days were lost through industrial disputes. Between June 1970 and the end of August 1972, 42,665,000 man-days were lost. While pensioners, the unemployed and families on the poverty line were suffering from the effects of rising prices and inflation, tax concessions in successive Budgets benefited the better off.

All this was grist to Wilson's mill and he made the most

of it. Of his many 'Heath-bashing' speeches, I select the one he made to the Blackpool conference in 1972:

Whatever contradictions and policy reversals we have seen without shame, without a blush, on one thing Mr Heath has shown utter consistency and let us not here rob him of his laurels. He has shown utter and systematic consistency in the breach of the solemn pledges, without which the Conservatives would never have become the Government ... What the British people now realise is that all his pledges on prices and the cost of living were made by a man who knew when he made them that they could not be honoured. So it is not a question of incompetence – it is a question of deliberate deceit. And that, even more than incompetence, has been the distinguishing, continuing feature equally of his Government.

Yet, despite broken promises and rising prices, there was no swing of public opinion towards the Labour Party. The Gallup poll between May 1971 and May 1972 showed a slight drop in Labour's lead – from 9 per cent to 6 per cent, and a fall in Wilson's own rating from 61 to 45 per cent though he was still ahead of Heath. Nearly three out of four people questioned regarded the Labour Party as 'divided' as compared to the Tories.

Normally, at the half-way mark in a government's term of office, the Opposition party can expect to do well in by-elections. Two years after Labour's 1966 victory, by-elections produced a string of Conservative gains, including some seats which Labour could have expected to hold. Some, but not all of the lost constituencies, were regained in 1970. In a few cases the swing to the Tories was as high as 18 per cent and Labour consistently lagged in the opinion polls at this time. It was the same when the Tories were in office under Macmillan. The Liberals were the immediate beneficiaries of public discontent, with the spectacular win of Orpington by Eric Lubbock in March 1962, but after that Labour began to pick up and won several by-elections in a row, as well as showing a steady improvement in the opinion polls.

If this same pattern had been repeated two-and-a-half years after the 1970 election the Labour Party could have expected to hold Rochdale, regain Uxbridge and make a good showing in Sutton and Cheam. Instead, as in Orpington, the Liberals swept the board at Rochdale and at Sutton and Cheam where they had a swing of nearly 40 per cent. Labour's vote at Uxbridge dropped from nearly 20,000 to 13,000 and their candidate at Sutton and Cheam lost his deposit (7 December 1972).

Admittedly, there were special factors in all three cases. Admittedly, by-elections are not a reliable guide to general elections. There tends to be a low turn-out and people cast their votes on irrelevant issues, or abstain in protest against politicians in general. But having said that, it must be recognised that the by-elections in the autumn and winter of 1972 were very serious set-backs for the Labour Party.

The inquests began the very same night. Lord George Brown exploded when he heard the results: 'The nation, dissatisfied as it is, quite properly, with the Conservative Government simply will not have the Labour Party, my party, with its present policies, present associations, present leadership. We must either change our present associations and policies, or the leaders associated with these must make way for other leaders who will, who can, make the change.'

The Times commented: 'If Labour cannot recover Uxbridge more than two years after a general election they have to change themselves radically if they are to stand a credible chance of winning a general election held in the next year or two.'

Anthony Crosland admitted: 'We did badly and everyone knows it. Now the worst reaction to this failure is the sort of panicky, apocalyptic defeatism displayed by George Brown.'

'The voters,' he said 'know what we are against; they don't know what we are for ... They are asking what we stand for now.'

Badly shaken by the results and realising the possibility that Heath might call an election in 1973 in order to cash in on Labour's disarray, the party leaders put a brave face on the defeat. 'No panic' became the order of the day. Harold Wilson himself confidently predicted that Labour would win the next election, whenever it came, and claimed that the party was more united against the Tories than at any time in the past twenty years. Dick Crossman denied that there was any leadership crisis and Chief Whip Bob Mellish, a loyal Wilson man, said that the Leader's position inside the movement was 'as strong as it ever has been and I think he is a very worthy leader of the party'. By contrast, Norman Atkinson, a Tribune group MP, warned that the party was heading for its 'biggest bust-up' if the leadership continued to ignore the wishes of the rank and file. 'At present Labour's front-bench spokesmen behave like a posse of do-it-yourself demonstrators, each doing his or her own thing.'

Within a few months the post-Uxbridge gloom had lifted and a new mood was discernible both inside and outside the House. This can be attributed to three factors. First, the end (for the time being at any rate) of the public bickering over Europe, with Britain's entry an accomplished fact. Second, the troubles on the Conservative back benches over Heath's dramatic conversion to statutory control over wages. Had their election manifesto, 'A better tomorrow' not categorically stated: 'We utterly reject the philosophy of compulsory wage control'? And had it not pledged that the manifesto's promises were not 'made only to be broken ... The last conservative Government kept all its promises. So will the next'? Was this not an insidious form of socialism creeping into Conservative philosophy, as Enoch Powell suggested? Peregrine Worsthorne summed up the dilemma *(The Sunday Telegraph,* 21 January 1973): 'Mr Heath is not only appealing to the Tory Party to back him in implementing this Socialist policy. He is saying that it is the duty of every citizen to do likewise. So now we have a Tory Prime Minister not only committing his party to make Socialist policies successful, but also seeking to harness the whole nation's patriotic enthusiasm behind this endeavour.' The policy, he warned, could only damage the Conservatives' electoral chances and promote the cause of the Labour Party.

The third factor which led to an upsurge in Labour's morale in January–February 1973 was Wilson's own 'comeback'. He re-established himself with one sparkling performance in Parliament and with thoughtful speeches in the country about Labour's future policy.

But the results of the by-elections, announced on 1 March, dealt a fresh blow to the more sanguine expectations that a lasting recovery was on the way. Dick Taverne, who had resigned the party Whip after a bitter disagreement with his local Labour Party over Europe and other issues, scored a victory at Lincoln as a 'democratic Labour' candidate, polling 21,967 votes compared with the 8,776 votes of the official, left-wing Labour candidate. The Conservative candidate, a right-wing Monday Club supporter, came third with 6,616 votes. At Dundee the official Labour man had a majority of 1,141, being closely run by a Scottish Nationalist. At Chester-le-Street, a safe Labour seat, a 20,000 majority was turned into a majority of just over 7,000, with the Liberals running second. The Tory lost his deposit.

At the same time a Gallup Poll *(The Daily Telegraph,* 15 March) showed a drop in Labour's lead over the Conservatives from 9 to 4 per cent, and a fall in Wilson's own rating from 44 per cent in December to 41 per cent.

All three by-elections, showing evidence of the continuing growth of the anti-party vote, caused fresh heart-searching among the party leadership and also threatened a new division within the movement. Roy Jenkins, speaking at Oxford, discounted the idea of a centre party alignment, but spoke frankly on Labour's malaise: 'There is something very wrong indeed with an opposition party which in mid term and in the winter of the Government's discontent cannot do better than this,' he said, listing three reasons for the public disillusionment with the major parties: boredom and dislike of slanging-matches; cynicism about easily-made promises; and the adoption of different sets of standards in politics and in ordinary life. There was, he said, a tiny minority, with an influence out of all proportion to its numbers, which was prepared 'to put the country to the misery of complete national failure'. 'Unless we make it clear that this catastrophic view in no way affects our policy-making, we might as well say goodbye to power for a generation ... It is time we started talking sense to the British people.'

Roy Jenkins, as always, had a good press reception, but was denounced by the left wing. Thus Barbara Castle accused the right of 'starting up all these old rows all over again. Let there be no mistake about who is trying to destroy our present unity,' she thundered. She was getting 'sick and tired of the attempt of some who pre-empt for themselves all the claims of probity, courage and consistency'.

The threatened renewed outbreak of conflict was hastily played down by the party leadership and by the middle-of-the-road MPs, of the same type that had formed the 'keep calm' group during the Bevanite days. Harold Wilson, whose own leadership came under fire and who appeared to turn an almost Attlee-like blind eye to internal rows, declined to comment on the Jenkins-Castle argument. 'Everyone must speak as he feels right in the situation ... We have our arguments out in public. Rather too much for comfort, but that is one of the consequences of being a democratic party,' he said. And his deputy leader, Edward Short, claimed that, so far from falling apart, the party was in excellent shape. The general desire all round was to damp down the smouldering flames.

II

The Wilson Governments

Notwithstanding its precarious hold in Parliament, where it had an overall majority of four, the fifth Labour Government under Harold Wilson got off to a flying start.[1] Wilson, in a TV broadcast on the night the results were known, declared: 'I want to make it quite clear that this will not affect our ability to govern. Having been charged with the duties of Government, we intend to carry out those duties ... Over the whole field of government, there will be many changes which we have been given a mandate by you to carry out. We intend to fulfil that mandate.'

The party had fought the 1964 election largely on its pledge to end 'stop-go' economic policies and to plan for sustained growth. Wilson was popular with the public and had a 20 per cent lead in the opinion polls over Sir Alec Douglas-Home. There was a general desire to give Labour the benefit of the doubt and a chance to work out its economic plans.

The first step was the creation of the Department of Economic Affairs, charged, as Wilson put it, with the task of fundamentally reconstructing and modernising industry, and providing a counter-weight to the all-powerful Treasury. The legend that the DEA was born in a taxi between the St Ermin's Hotel and the House of Commons does not stand up to examination. The creation of such a department had been in Wilson's mind since 1963. The only thing that happened in that taxi was that George Brown was offered, and accepted, the job of Secretary of State for Economic Affairs.

Brown was ecstatic and indefatigable. He has written

[1] See Harold Wilson, *The Labour Government, 1964–70* (Weidenfeld/ Michael Joseph 1971).

that the creation of the DEA 'was meant to be, and might have been, the greatest contribution of the Labour Party to the recasting of the machinery of government to meet the needs of the twentieth century . . . . a wholly novel form of national social accountancy to replace the orthodox financial accountancy by which the Treasury has always dominated British life'.[1] He recruited top economists and industrialists to man and advise the department and made himself highly unpopular by poaching civil servants from other Whitehall departments. There was a proliferation of 'little Neddies' for nearly every industry and the foundations were laid for the Industrial Reorganisation Corporation, to promote mergers and strengthen efficiency.

George Brown's first achievement just before Christmas 1964 was to draw up a Declaration of Intent in which employers and union leaders pledged their co-operation in the voluntary restraint of prices and incomes and in removing obstacles to greater efficiency. It was a lofty declaration and though in the end it turned out about as meaningless as Chamberlain's 'peace with honour' scrap of paper after Munich, produced a seasonable atmosphere of peace and goodwill. Later, Brown set up the National Board for Prices and Incomes, with Aubrey Jones, a former Conservative Minister, as its chairman. The Board was limited by not being able to initiate its own investigations, and having to wait for a reference from the Government, but it became an essential part of the economic furniture until it was dismantled by the Tory Government. Brown described the prices and incomes policy as 'the key to an economically growing and socially just society'. The consent of the TUC was secured by an overwhelming majority in April 1965 – the only dissenters being the Transport Union.

George Brown followed up his success with the preparation of a National Plan, published the following September. This was an ambitious project, envisaging a 25 per cent growth rate by 1970 and setting targets for every major industry. It was to be a shining example of practical socialism in action, the instrument for changing the economic and social structure of British society. It was also to be realistic

[1] George Brown, *In My Way* (Gollancz and Penguin 1971/2).

and feasible. Brown told the party conference in 1964: 'This will be no paper plan for the pigeon-holes, but a solidly-based, carefully worked-out project, with the full weight of the Government and of both sides of industry.'

In the event, the Plan was a casualty of successive economic and financial crises. The rate of growth planned for 25 per cent was only 14 per cent; there was insufficient investment and the expected increases in productivity and in the rate of exports did not materialise. Brown later attributed the disappointing results, not to any weaknesses in the Plan itself, but to the failure of the Government to give it priority and the triumph of orthodox Treasury financiers over the fledgling DEA.

The Labour Government inherited an appallingly difficult financial situation, as its spokesmen never tired of reminding the public. The 'twelve years of Tory misrule' had ended with a deficit in the balance of payments, running at an annual rate of £800 million and sterling was under severe pressure. To meet the situation Wilson imposed a surcharge of 15 per cent on imports of manufactures and semi-manufactures, thereby incurring the anger of the EFTA countries.

The obvious course would have been devaluation, but this was 'ruled out by deliberate decision'. With a tiny majority and with vivid memories of the effect of the Cripps devaluation on public opinion, Wilson refused to countenance this course. 'I was convinced and my colleagues agreed that to devalue could have the most dangerous consequences.'[1] Political considerations thus over-rode what would have made economic sense and the Government, guided by a misplaced type of patriotism, took the line that the pound must be able to look the dollar in the face. Devaluation from then on became an 'unmentionable' subject.

It is easy to understand why, with its knife-edge majority and in the tense political climate of 1964–6 the Government decided against devaluation. It is less easy to understand why, once it had secured a handsome majority of 97 seats in the 1966 election, it did not take the plunge, especially

[1] Harold Wilson, *The Labour Government, 1964–70* (Michael Joseph 1971).

after the financial crisis of July. George Brown, Roy Jenkins and Anthony Crosland were in favour of devaluing; Wilson and his Chancellor Callaghan were against. Instead, the Government decided on a massive programme of deflation. Brown actually submitted his resignation in protest at the deflation which would effectively strangle his beloved National Plan, and only withdrew it after extreme pressure from his friends in the House.

Professor Wilfred Beckerman, who at one time served with the DEA, has written: 'The natural – though still unpleasant – policy choice was to devalue. They did not. Why not is one of the major political puzzles of the 1960s.'[1] His own verdict: 'Failure to devalue the pound earlier was the major cause of the economic difficulties throughout the period of the Labour Government and an earlier devaluation would have had numerous beneficial effects.'

R. H. S. Crossman, who was a member of the Cabinet throughout, later described this delay as one of the Government's two big blunders, the other being the failure to withdraw sooner from East of Suez.

The deflationary package and cut-backs introduced on 20 July 1966, together with the imposition of a freeze on prices and wages, resulted in producing very different relationships with the unions from those which had prevailed at the time of the Declaration of Intent. The freeze was far more rigid than the hated 'pay pause' of Selwyn Lloyd. There was a complete standstill on pay increases, to be followed by six months of severe restraint, with a zero norm; prices would be held, apart from rises due to import prices and taxes, and there would be a 12 months standstill on dividends. Social service spending was exempted.

The TUC General Council adopted an attitude of 'reluctant acquiescence' but Frank Cousins who had resigned as Minister of Technology on the issue, Clive Jenkins and other militants kept up a relentless opposition. Cousins's view, expressed in Parliament, was: 'It is a bad

[1] Wilfred Beckerman (ed.), *The Labour Government's Economic Record, 1964–70* (Duckworth 1972).

Bill ... It is a move to make the trade union movement an adjunct of the Government. I don't think you can have free trade unions in a social democratic society when the intention of the Bill is to tell the unions what they can and cannot do.'

The critics failed to stop, or alter, the Bill which became law on 12 August. Part I gave statutory recognition to the Prices and Incomes Board; Part II gave force to the 'early warning' system, requiring notification of proposed increases and references to the Board. The voluntary element was thus still preserved, but Part IV gave statutory force to the standstill and provided for fines of up to £500 for any breaches, or attempted breaches through strikes. This section was brought into force in October, following the refusal of the newspaper proprietors to delay a cost of living increase to print workers. Three Ministers left the Labour Party conference to fly from Brighton to Balmoral to seek the Queen's assent to the Order.

The cuts, estimated to save about £500 million, were even tougher than those imposed by Cripps in the 1940s. This was 'stop-go' with a vengeance. The fury of the Midlands car workers who demonstrated outside the Prime Minister's hotel at Brighton to protest against redundancies and sackings, was typical of the widespread dismay which swept through the movement. Was this to be 1931 all over again? Were the international bankers and the 'gnomes of Zurich' to control the destinies of the Labour Government and compel it to adopt Tory policies? Michael Foot eloquently summed up the position as the left saw it 'We are not our own masters ... I say, any Government worth its salt, particularly a Labour Government, would do everything in its power to escape from the position of humiliating dependence as swiftly as possible ... We shall not beat this economic crisis with the rusty weapons of our opponents. We will not solve this problem by dressing ourselves in the deflationary clothes of the Tories ... We have to carry our policies into the innermost citadels of finance and defence and foreign policy.'

Foot won a resounding ovation, but the NEC statement endorsing the Government's economic policies was carried by a three to two majority, after a straight-from-the-shoulder appeal for loyalty by the Prime Minister.

The freeze was successful in its objective of stabilising wages. The index of weekly wage rates stood still for five months and the retail price index moved up only one point.

After the disastrous effect on the balance of trade of the seamen's strike in May a surplus was recorded in the last quarter of the year. The pound was healthier than for some time past.

But the lull was deceptive, and the political price of the improvement in sterling was heavy. From the spring of 1967 nothing seemed to go right for the Government. Public opinion polls showed a drop in its standing, and even Wilson's own ratings fell. A series of by-elections resulted in increased Tory majorities in two seats, a Tory win in Glasgow Pollock and – the most unkindest cut of all – the loss of Rhondda West to the Welsh Nationalists. The Tories swept the board in the local elections and even captured London, which had been under Labour control since 1934. Unemployment began to creep up. From a state of relatively full employment, with a national average of about 1 to 1½ per cent of the labour force, it rose to 2 to 2½ per cent and the July 1967 figure was the highest for that month for twenty-seven years. The relaxation of the Prices and Incomes Act, when 'moderation' succeeded 'severe restraint' resulted in renewed inflation, which contributed to the loss of foreign confidence in Britain's economy. The TUC that year turned against the Government's policy.

There were troubles abroad. The civil war in Nigeria and the six-day Israel-Arab war which closed the Suez Canal adversely affected the balance of payments. The impasse over Rhodesia continued and the Vietnamese war dragged on.

Wilson had found it much easier to manage the Parliamentary party when he could count his majority on the fingers of one hand. Labour MPs grew increasingly restive and worried about Government policies and the lack of contact. After forty-two MPs abstained on the Defence White Paper, the Prime Minister read the riot act. With, for him, unusual tetchiness and loss of cool, he warned 'Every dog is allowed one bite, but a different view is taken of a dog that goes on biting all the time. He may not get his licence renewed when it falls due.' There were serious and damaging dock strikes in London and Liverpool in the autumn and the balance of payment continued to deteriorate; the country's reserves were draining away at an alarming rate.

So at last, on Sunday 19 November, the decision to devalue was announced and the pound dropped from $2.80 to $2.40. Its impact was not immediate, and it was not until early in 1969 that the balance moved firmly into surplus.

James Callaghan could not be expected to preside over a policy in which he did not believe and he swapped places with Roy Jenkins, the Home Secretary, who had long been an advocate of devaluation. Other Cabinet changes were on the way. Michael Stewart was moved from the DEA to the Foreign Office when George Brown finally resigned in March 1968. The DEA gradually petered out (and with it the National Plan) and was finally wound up in 1969. Many Foreign Office officials breathed a sigh of relief when Stewart, with his quiet rather schoolmasterly manner, returned to the Foreign Office and the somewhat turbulent and temperamental rule of George Brown was ended. The most important change in home affairs was the appointment in April of Barbara Castle to the Ministry of Labour, re-named Department of Employment and Productivity. Ray Gunter, a former President of the railway clerks' union, had become attached to what he called his 'bed of nails' and deeply resented being moved from Labour to the Ministry of Power. He resigned a few months later, after a bitter attack on Wilson's leadership and complaints that the Government was being run by a handful of intellectuals who knew nothing at all about the unions. With his departure, following those of Cousins, Douglas Houghton and George Brown, the Cabinet was almost entirely bereft of trade unionists.

This lack of contact with the unions contributed to the worsening of relations within the movement and the eventual collapse of the Government. Attlee and Cripps might be classed as middle-class intellectuals, but the rock-like figure of Ernest Bevin provided a constant safeguard of trade union interests and a guide to their attitudes. Wilson had no such support.

Barbara Castle brought in a bill to continue the prices and incomes policy for a further period and to stiffen the delaying powers. She then became immersed in plans to curb industrial unrest which had been mounting at an alarming rate. In 1966 2,398,000 working days had been lost in strikes. In 1968 the total was nearly twice as high with 4,690,000 days lost. Things were even worse in 1969 when 6,846,000 days were lost. It was obvious to Barbara that something must be done. She was used to getting her own way and as Minister of Transport had pushed through her breathalyser legislation in the face of stiff opposition. But she did not reckon with the effect of trade union hostility. It seemed as if an irresistible force was meeting an immovable object, but in the end the immovable object won.

The TUC argued vehemently that further legislation was unnecessary, because of the Donovan Royal Commission on trade unions, which had upheld the voluntary principle and rejected the idea of legislative action. Neither Mrs Castle nor Harold Wilson were impressed. They could read the statistics and could work out trends. They could see the damaging effects stoppages, particularly in the car industry, were having on the jobs of other workers and on the attitude of the general public. 'Strike after strike, frustrating the effort of Government, signalling the question-mark to those industrialists who are attracted by the inducements the Government provide and who are planning establishing themselves here,' was how Wilson reacted to a Ford dispute on Merseyside.

Public opinion was in favour of action to curb strikes and was becoming increasingly hostile to the trade unions.

This was the background to the 'In place of strife' White Paper[1] – a title devised by Barbara's journalist husband Ted – which evoked the memory of Bevan's 'In place of

[1] See Peter Jenkins, *The Battle of Downing Street* (Charles Knight 1971).

fear'. Published in January 1969 the White Paper made provision for the legal rights and recognition of trade unionists, but contained clauses against unconstitutional strikes, including a conciliation 'pause' of twenty-eight days and giving the Secretary of State authority to impose a settlement in an inter-union dispute and order a strike ballot if thought necessary. All three proposals went far beyond the recommendations of the Royal Commission.

George Woodcock who was still TUC general secretary was not at first unfavourable. 'I don't think there is anything in this to which the unions can fundamentally object,' he is reported to have said. But the TUC General Council reacted violently against the plan and drew up its counter-proposals in 'Programme for action', vesting the General Council with greater authority to intervene in inter-union disputes. This programme was later approved at a special conference, but neither Wilson nor Barbara Castle thought it would be effective.

They urged Victor Feather, who had succeeded Woodcock, to get the General Council to assume direct powers to deal with unofficial strikes, but the TUC refused to budge.

In the meantime there was intense activity in Parliament. About fifty-three Labour MPs, mostly from the trade union group, voted against the Government when the White Paper was debated and another forty abstained. Douglas Houghton, the PLP chairman, warned Wilson that the party might disintegrate if he pushed ahead with this highly explosive legislation. There was a growing move to force Wilson's resignation and one MP collected the names of about ninety-five Members, in order that a special meeting 'to consider the leadership question' should be called. After one stormy meeting of the PLP, Wilson noted in his diary 'All hell was let loose. The left was inflamed by Bob Mellish. Meanwhile the professional WMG (Wilson must go) group was also at work.'[1] Vic Feather, referring to the move to unseat Wilson, declared 'The TUC has not had a part in any political shenanigans at Westminster or else-where.' The attempted putsch was abandoned when it

[1] Wilson, op. cit., p. 646.

leaked prematurely to the press, but the storm continued. A flood of resolutions from union branches and local parties poured in and the National Executive carried a resolution against the industrial relations policy. Callaghan, though a member of the Cabinet, voted for it. As party Treasurer he had kept in close touch with the unions and realised the damaging effects the Castle proposals would have on their willingness to provide funds for the next election. He had been excluded from the Inner Cabinet, and the handling of the Bill was left to Barbara Castle, Harold Wilson and Roy Jenkins.

Wilson, whose loyalty to Barbara Castle was unshakeable, was resolute, and pointed to the fact that over 70 per cent of the public, according to an opinion poll, backed the Government. The Bill, he said, was 'essential to our economic recovery, essential to the balance of payments, essential to full employment ... the passage of this Bill is essential to its (the Government's) continuance in office'. He dismissed the plots against his leadership. 'I know what's going on. I'm going on,' he told a May day rally in London.

In the end, under mounting pressure and in a position of increasing isolation, he and Barbara Castle were forced to climb down and drop the penal clauses. A face-saving formula was found. The TUC gave a 'solemn and binding' undertaking that the General Council would act in the event of unconstitutional disputes and would deal with unions which did not comply under their Rule 13. This declaration of intent was to prove no more effective than that on prices and incomes but Wilson said that the unions, under threat of legislation, had moved further in a few weeks than in the previous forty years.

When one looks at Wilson's shaky position in the summer of 1969 it is remarkable indeed that he should have recovered his prestige and popularity to such an extent as to embark on a general election, exactly a year after the climb-down on industrial relations. This was as much due to the failure of Ted Heath to make any impact as to Wilson's own performance. But with the steady improvement in the balance of trade and the avoidance of controversial issues in the 1969–70 Parliamentary session, the Labour Party regained its unity, if not its élan. The knowledge of an impending election invariably has a unifying effect.

The Conservative lead in the opinion polls fell steadily in the second half of 1969 and, despite a series of disappointing by-election results, Labour made a good showing in the polls. This continued lead, as well as the improved economic situation, decided the Prime Minister to go to the country in June 1970, rather than wait till the end of the Government's term of office in October. The fear of another economic crisis in the autumn was another compelling factor. Being wise after the event, he probably would have been better advised to wait until October, avoid the holiday period and allow the party's election machine to get into top gear.

The 1970 campaign was fought almost exclusively on the Government's economic record with the slogan 'Now Britain's strong, let's make her great to live in'.

Wilson dominated the campaign in almost Presidential fashion, with frequent TV appearances and a series of 'meet the people' tours. Most of the pollsters and punters predicted a Labour victory up to the very last moment, which made the actual result even harder for Labour supporters to bear. The Tories were returned with a majority of twenty-nine seats and a national swing to them of 4.7 per cent. Labour lost seventy-four seats, among them some held by prominent Ministers. There was a low turnout, about 72 per cent, and there was no sign that the newly enfranchised eighteen–twenty-one year-olds showed much interest in the fortunes of either party.[1]

So ended the sixth Labour Government.

[1] For an analysis of the election campaign and results see David Butler and M. Pinto-Duschinsky, *The British General Election of 1970* (Macmillan 1971).

III

The record

Future historians will pass judgment on the record of the Labour Governments between 1964 and 1970. Many analyses and appraisals have already been made.[1] The main theme is inevitably disappointment at the failure to advance towards the long-term objective of changing society. The promises of 1964 foundered on the rocks of economic crisis. Obsessed with the problems of maintaining the parity of the pound and closing the trade gap, the Government seemed to many of its supporters to have lost its sense of purpose.

It is however only fair to point out the achievements, as well as the failures of the Government.

Strenuous efforts were made to protect the weaker members of society from the worst effect of the economic crises. In the very first Queen's Speech in 1964 increases in old age pensions and other benefits were announced. The fact that, owing to administrative difficulties, they were not brought into effect in time for Christmas caused dismay among delegates to the 1964 weekend 'victory' conference, especially since the House had just voted to increase MPs' own salaries.

Successive adjustments were made in social security benefits. Between 1964 and 1969 expenditure on social services (excluding housing) increased by 65 per cent. The cost of supplementary benefits and family allowances more than doubled. But the value of additional cash benefits was steadily eroded by inflation.

Another form of increased, if indirect, benefits was provided through higher spending on health and education.

[1] See Wilfred Beckerman (ed.), *The Labour Government's Economic Record* (Duckworth 1972). Also Peter Townsend and Nicholas Bosanquet, *Labour and Inequality: sixteen Fabian essays* (Fabian Society 1972).

Expenditure on health increased from 4.2 per cent of the gross national product in 1964 to 5 per cent in 1969, while that on education rose from 4.8 per cent in 1964 to 5.9 per cent in 1968. Although it did nothing about the public schools, beyond setting up a Commission of investigation, the Government went ahead with ambitious plans for setting up comprehensive schools and ending the eleven plus examination. More teachers were trained and more children stayed longer at school. The number of university students increased (not everybody would agree that this was an advantage!) and the Open University, originally regarded as something of a joke, became an accepted and popular feature in the educational world. Public support for the arts was increased, and it was said that Jennie Lee, who enjoyed Wilson's personal protection, was the only Minister whose budget escaped unscathed.

More money was spent on health and hospitals – the hospital building programme was exempted from cuts in 1968 – and some progress was made in developing health centres. At all costs the objective was that the National Health Service, the finest domestic achievement of the Attlee Government and a living monument to Nye Bevan's memory, must not be tampered with. Expenditure on health rose by £700 million during the Government's term of office. But the Government's policy did not escape criticism, particularly when it re-imposed prescription charges in 1968, and there were complaints about the failure to inject more democracy into hospital managements and to tackle the problem of mental health.

Housing is perhaps the biggest single problem facing national and local government. The Labour Government had set itself a target of 500,000 houses a year. This was not achieved, but as many as 2 million new houses were built while it was in office – about half of them in the local authority sector. Nearly half a million slums were cleared and local authorities were given grants for improving older properties. More New Towns were designated. The Land Commission, which was designed to provide a sufficient supply of land at controlled prices and thus prevent profiteering, was not a success. Its machinery was too slow and cumbersome. An

c

Urban Programme to help social development in the most deprived areas, was announced in 1968.

Labour's attitude to industry was equivocal. It needed the co-operation of the captains of industry in its plans for economic expansion, and in its prices and incomes policy, but there was still a traditional suspicion about the motives of capitalists. Wilson and Brown both accepted the existence of a mixed economy in Britain, and there was only one new Act of nationalisation – that of steel. This long-promised and long-delayed measure went through Parliament in 1967 without much fuss, compared with the furore which had attended the initial nationalisation Act in the 1940s. In general the Government encouraged and assisted the nationalised industries to become more efficient and up-to-date, but relations between Ministers and some of the Boards' chairmen were frequently strained. Lord Robens, at the Coal Board, attacked the Whitehall planners for allowing the coal industry to run down to a dangerously low level.

The main instrument of control over private industry was the Industrial Reorganisation Corporation, which came under George Brown and the DEA. It was given power to 'promote or assist' the reorganisation of industrial development.

The IRC operated mainly by persuasion, backed up where appropriate by loans and in some cases, for example in the electrical and electronic industries, by direct intervention . . .

The DEA was not the only department where they burned midnight oil. Down the road at Millbank, in Vickers' sky-scraper building, Frank Cousins, Minister of Technology was building up a power-house. Having started the department with himself, Lord Snow and three other men, he was due to become virtual 'Supremo' when engineering and ship-building were added to his technological empire. (He resigned before the move actually took place.) The saving of the British computer industry from imminent collapse was perhaps the Ministry's most valuable achievement. For the rest it sponsored developments in advanced machine tools and standardisation, made grants for research and helped small engineering firms with technical advice. It was hardly the 'white heat' of Wilson's scientific revolution, but the

Ministry made a useful contribution to the economy, first under Cousins and later under Anthony Wedgwood Benn.

The Labour Government failed to arrest the national growth in unemployment, but, as a result of its regional policies of pumping assistance into the development areas, it managed to reduce the hitherto widening gap between employment in the richer and the poorer areas.

In labour relations, the Government speeded up the pace of reform in such areas as training, redundancy and labour mobility and dock decasualisation. It established the Donovan Royal Commission on trade unions and employers' associations and, following its recommendation, set up the Commission on Industrial Relations to advise both sides of industry on how to improve collective bargaining procedures. It encouraged productivity agreements negotiated at shop-floor level and continued to exercise its traditional mediation and conciliation functions. In the very last year of its office it introduced an Equal Pay Act, providing for equal pay between men and women by December 1975 – though, according to all the available evidence, progress towards this goal has been painfully slow and the traditional definition of 'women's work' is being applied to prevent any serious negotiations in many firms and industries. There was, however, no restructuring of the industrial relations system and the two attempts at Government intervention – the prices and incomes policy and the labour relations plan – had to be abandoned as a result of trade union opposition.

At the Home Office Roy Jenkins piloted through a number of enlightened, if controversial, measures in the sphere of prison reform, civil liberties and race relations. Private MPs were helped to introduce bills reforming the homosexual, abortion and divorce laws, and capital punishment was abolished on a free vote of Parliament.

All this gave great delight to liberal opinion but created anger among many Conservatives who protested about the introduction of a 'permissive' society. Jenkins preferred to use the word 'civilised'. By contrast the Government's immigration measures and treatment of the Kenyan Asians were bitterly opposed by the liberal elements in the party.

There are differing views about the extent to which the

Labour Government was able to achieve greater social equality. According to Professor Beckerman, 'Some progress was made to achieve the goal that, more than any other, characterised the Labour Party's economic policy, namely greater equality of incomes. This arose largely through the increase in benefits, in cash and in kind, to the poorer groups in society, though efforts were also made in taxation policy and in prices and incomes policy to improve the relative position of the lower paid.' In the same book, Michael Stewart (of University College London) concludes that 'To have promoted a measurable improvement in the distribution of income against the background of the deplorably slow rate of growth of output permitted by its macro-economic policies was one of the Labour Government's main achievements'.

The Fabians, however, come to the opposite conclusion. The record, they say, provides a 'gloomy picture . . . confirms the inability of the Government to use its power on behalf of the weaker members of the community'.

The sociologist Peter Townsend goes even further. 'The Government did not diminish inequalities of income, or did not reduce them much . . . Considerable poverty remained among the families of the low-paid, old people, the unemployed, the disabled and fatherless families. Resources were not steered towards the fulfilment of social objectives by means of what by international and historical standards would have been a really dramatic expansion of social services. It is impossible not to feel a sense of dismay.'

The Fabians may be unduly harsh in their strictures and have perhaps not taken sufficient account of the Government's economic dilemma. But there is ample evidence to show that the gap between the well-off and the poor continued to widen during the second half of the sixties. Roy Jenkins[1] estimated that at the end of the 1960s about 2 million people were living below the poverty line (as defined by the Supplementary Benefit scales) while another 4.6 million were receiving benefit and a further 4 million had incomes only just above the line. Altogether 10.6 million

[1] Roy Jenkins, *What Matters Now* (Collins/Fontana 1972).

people had incomes near the poverty line – about one-fifth of the population.

A remarkable omission from Labour's policies was the absence of a tax on wealth, which had been much talked about, especially in Hugh Gaitskell's day. There was a capital gains tax, introduced in 1965, and there was a series of new taxes, as well as a tightening up on tax evasion, but, as the Fabians point out, 'It is manifest that inequalities of ownership have not been seriously impugned.' There was a very slight redistribution – in 1968, 24 per cent of net wealth was owned by the top 1 per cent of wealth owners, compared with 25 per cent in 1964, and the share of the bottom 50 per cent increased from 8 per cent to 10 per cent.

One cannot help asking how Tawney would have viewed this marginal change brought about under a Labour Government with an overwhelming majority and at a time of immense technological potential for raising living standards all round. Michael Young, founder of the Consumers' Association and at one time research secretary at Transport House, said in a Rita Hinden memorial lecture in November 1972 that the 'tragic failure of the Labour Government to do more than tinker with the problems of social justice' ranked in his mind along with Munich as 'one of the two greatest political setbacks in this country' in his lifetime.

Another disappointment was the failure of the Government to live up to its early promise on overseas aid.

Harold Wilson had often spoken and written in passionate terms about the need to help the developing countries and to combat world poverty, and Labour had promised in its 1964 manifesto to 'give a dynamic lead in this vital field'. A special Ministry of Overseas Development was established, under the leadership of Barbara Castle, who was given a seat in the Cabinet. With Sir Andrew Cohen at her right hand, she prepared far-reaching programmes and cut through a great deal of the international red tape which was impeding the effectiveness of aid. But Barbara was moved to the Ministry of Transport in December 1965. Soon after, the MOD no longer ranked a seat in the Cabinet and overseas aid fell victim to the recurrent cuts, as the balance of payments worsened – there were no votes in it, anyhow. In the end less Government aid was given than when Labour assumed office – the proportion of net aid fell to 0.39 per cent of the national product in 1969 compared with 0.48 in 1965. No wonder that Messrs Seers and Streeten, in Beckerman's book, conclude: 'Labour's record was discreditable, especially in contrast to the promises before the election (which some of us were naive enough to believe).'

The falling off in overseas aid undoubtedly contributed to a loss of the Government's prestige among the newly independent nations of Africa and Asia. So did its failure to reach a settlement with Ian Smith or to impose effective sanctions on Rhodesia.

It was not a happy period in international affairs. British entry into Europe was blocked by de Gaulle. The continuing war in Vietnam and Britain's refusal to condemn the Americans led to violent demonstrations and protests from various left-wing groups. There was a perpetual state of tension in the Middle East and on top of everything religious conflict flared up in Northern Ireland. Jim Callaghan handled the situation with great skill, but after nearly four years, the Irish problem was as intractable and tragic as ever.

IV

The anatomy of the party

In 1970, as after previous election defeats, there were demands for an overhaul of the Labour Party machinery and organisation, which had failed to pull out the maximum Labour vote or appeal to a wider public. In these inevitable 'What went wrong?' inquests, insufficient organisation is often blamed for defeat.

This happened in 1955, when, after a tepid campaign, Labour did badly and lost over $1\frac{1}{2}$ million votes compared with 1951. The National Executive Committee set up a sub committee, headed by Harold Wilson, 'to enquire into all aspects of party organisation which directly affect the efficiency of our electoral machinery at national, regional, constituency and ward (or village) level'. The Wilson Committee reported that it was 'deeply shocked' at the state of the organisation in many parts of the country. 'Compared with our opponents, we are still at the penny-farthing stage in a jet-propelled age, and our machine at that is rusty and deteriorating with age.' It made various proposals for modernisation, such as increases in the staff, better equipment and improvements in the organisation in marginal constituencies. But the party did not want to be propelled into the jet age.

When the Wilson report was discussed at a private session at the Margate conference in October, many delegates resented its criticisms. (The device of a private session, incidentally, usually ensures that its proceedings get the maximum coverage in the morrow's papers and Margate 1955 was no exception.) Aneurin Bevan attacked the report, declaring that what was wrong was not faulty organisation, but lack of policy, which was barely indistinguishable from that of the Tories. Sam Watson, the Durham miners' leader, had earlier boasted that Labour had 'the finest political machine of any political party in Europe' and he, and other traditionalists, were angry at the slurs on the efficiency of the General secretary, Morgan Phillips. In view of the opposition to the report from both right-and left-wing quarters, it is not surprising that comparatively little was done to implement it.

Inquests and investigations, both official and unofficial, continued. In 1962 the Fabian Society returned to the attack with a critical pamphlet, *The Mechanics of Victory*, and as recently as 1965 *Socialist Commentary*, the middle-of-the-road monthly journal, published a supplement, harking back to the Wilson report under the title 'Our Penny-farthing Machine'. This formed the basis of a new organisation 'Plan for an efficient Party machine' led by a former Transport House official, Jim Northcott.

The most recent official investigation was the Executive's sub-committee, headed by William Simpson, the foundry-man's leader (and 1972–3 party chairman). The Simpson committee, appointed in 1967, was mainly concerned as was the Wilson Committee, with internal organisation. Many of its recommendations were held over, because of the impending change in the general secretaryship.

In a recent Fabian pamphlet (June 1971), 'The Labour Party: an organisational study', a writer called for much more fundamental research into inter-party relationships and into the way in which local parties operate, rather than their formal and mechanical structure.

This is a never-ending debate. It raises such questions as: how important is organisation in general and local elections? How far can amateur effort be superseded by professional methods? Can the lack of professionalism be compensated for by the enthusiasm of volunteers? There is no easy answer, and everybody has his own theories.

Thus, Hugh Gaitskell, smarting under the unexpected election defeat of 1959, declined to blame the party organisa-tion for the failure. The machinery, he said at the special Blackpool conference in late November, was in 'far better' shape than it had been in 1955. It was not bad organisation or publicity, lack of central direction or too late a start that had caused the defeat. It was, he suggested, because Labour policies had not matched the 'significant changes in the economic and social background of politics'.

Gaitskell suggested that the time had come to bring up to date the party Constitution drawn up in 1918 and in particular to have another look at Clause Four, which states as its objective: 'To secure for the workers by hand or by brain the full fruits of their industry and the most equitable distribution thereof that may be possible upon the basis of the common ownership of the means of production, distribution and exchange.'

The bitter controversy which met his sincere, but ill-timed, suggestion is discussed in Chapter XI. At this stage, before going into questions of policies and principles, it may be useful to examine more closely the existing structure and organisation of the party.

The Constitution was drafted by Arthur Henderson, then secretary of the party, with the help of Sidney Webb, whose hand was detected in the inclusion of Clause Four. Their object was to weld the trade union and socialist elements of the movement into one party and for the first time provide an opportunity for individual membership in constituency organisations. Apart from periodic amendments, to bring the organisation up to date, the 1918 Constitution has remained fundamentally unchanged. It sets out in great detail the composition and structure of the party, conditions of membership, affiliation fees and voting arrangements.

For a party which usually regards itself as pragmatic, as distinct from the doctrinaire basis of Continental socialists, it sometimes seems strange that Labour should adhere so strictly to well-defined and detailed rules, and be so reluctant to change them.

THE PARTY CONFERENCE

'The annual conference of the Labour Party is the fountain of authority,' states an official handbook (*How the Labour Party Works*, 1971). The 1918 Constitution puts it: 'The work of the party shall be under the direction and control of the party conference,' and in Clause V, 'The party conference shall decide from time to time what specific proposals of legislative, financial or administrative reform shall be included in the party programme.'

The basis of representation at conference is as follows:

1   One delegate for every 5,000 members of affiliated unions or part thereof,
2   One delegate for every 5,000 individual members, or part thereof for constituency parties, plus an additional woman delegate where membership is over 1,500,
3   One delegate for each central party and for each federation,
4   *Ex officio* members, without the right to vote, are members of the NEC, the Parliamentary Labour Party, duly endorsed Labour candidates and the party secretary.

Conference meets once a year, at the beginning of October, for four and a half days, and is usually attended by about 1,500 delegates, *ex officio* members and agents, plus perhaps as many as 2–3,000 visitors, journalists and broadcasting staffs. The trade unions rarely take up their full quota of delegates and are often out-numbered by constituency delegates.

The vast majority of the resolutions on the agenda are submitted by constituency parties. These have to reach head office not later than twelve clear weeks before conference, so that in practice they tend to reflect concern about issues which may have become less topical when conference actually opens. Constituency delegates are usually mandated by their local parties on how to vote on major topics, though in some cases they are allowed a free hand. Union votes are sometimes cast on the basis of their own conference decisions, but frequently these are left to eve-of-conference delegate meetings.

The preliminary agenda is circulated to organisations for amendment and when it comes to conference is drastically pruned and subjected to a process known as 'compositing'. This often produces inordinately long and ambiguous motions. Movers of resolutions are allowed ten minutes and other speakers are limited to five, but there is no official time-limit on platform speakers who take up about a third of conference time. Consequently, many delegates return home with undelivered speeches in their pockets and a sense of frustration through their failure to catch the chairman's eye. The Simpson Committee reported that in 1966 there were 556 motions dealing with 83 subjects on the agenda and that decisions were made on only 25 subjects, but decided it could do nothing about the overloading of the agenda.

Trade union speakers generally take up relatively little conference time, but in the end, it is their votes that count. Voting strengths at the 1972 conference were as follows:

	Delegates	No. of organisations	Votes
Trade unions	610	55	5,562,000
Constituency & Central Labour parties	556	548	706,000
Socialist societies, Cooperative organisations and Federations	16	12	42,000
	1,182	615	6,310,000

In other words, the trade union vote amounts to almost 90 per cent of the total number cast.

THE NATIONAL EXECUTIVE COMMITTEE

The Party's National Executive Committee is elected annually by the conference. It is described in the Constitution as the 'administrative authority' of the party. It formulates policy, prepares statements and constitutional amendments, and submits resolutions to the conference; it controls finance and exercises discipline over errant party members.

The NEC consists of twenty-eight elected members, including the Treasurer, and *ex officio* the Leader and deputy Leader. (The deputy Leader was given a place in 1953 when by an ingenious formula proposed by the National Union of Seamen, a seat was found for Herbert Morrison who had been knocked off the Executive in 1952.)

There are four divisions – the trade unions elect twelve representatives, the constituency parties seven, and the socialist societies one, while the whole conference elects five women members and the Treasurer. The Simpson Committee recommended the abolition of the separate women's section as incompatible with modern trends, but this change was not accepted. Although Barbara Castle and Joan Lestor were returned in the constituency section in competition with the men, the Women's Advisory Committee did not want such a manifestation of Women's Lib on the NEC.

The secretary of the party has a seat but not a vote.

The voting pattern in the trade union section is usually fairly static, apart from changes in order of popularity, but the election of the seven constituency representatives and of the women members is fiercely competitive and gives rise to considerable excitement. The most dramatic elections were at Morecambe in 1952 when six of the seven constituency places were filled by Bevanite candidates. Dick Crossman and Ian Mikardo replaced the veteran leaders Herbert Morrison and Hugh Dalton. (Ironically it was Morrison who piloted through the constitutional reform in 1937 which gave separate representation to the constituencies.)

CONSTITUENCY LABOUR PARTIES

The brunt of keeping the party going in the country is borne by the constituency labour parties, which are officially described as 'the operative units of party activity'. They are based on Parliamentary constituency boundaries, and in urban districts are organised on the basis of wards, which correspond to local authority electoral areas. Most C.L.P.'s have separate sections for women and for young socialists. Local trade union branches are affiliated to them and trade unionists are always being pressed to join as individual members. Wards and affiliated organisations send delegates to the C.L.P. General Management Committee which is the controlling body and has its own elected executive and officers.

Local parties are in most respects autonomous. They raise their own funds, paying affiliation fees to the National

Executive, and run their own affairs. Provided they follow the rules they are usually left to their own devices by headquarters. Their effectiveness varies according to the calibre of their officers.

The main *raison d'être* of constituency parties is to mobilise support and votes at general and local elections. This includes canvassing, keeping records, distributing and producing literature, and organising polling day activities. David Butler, the Nuffield College psephologist and authority on elections, thinks that the importance of local organisation in affecting election results is overrated. It is true that the impact of TV and the press on election campaigns has tended to out-date the traditional methods of electioneering – people can follow events on the screen without bothering to go to meetings in their locality. At the same time, particularly in country districts, many voters appreciate the personal touch and are offended if they are not visited by the candidate, or if the election address does not reach them. In my own view, the amount of time and energy that goes into the writing, filling and distribution of election addresses is altogether out of proportion to the results achieved. Others would argue that it is all part of the democratic process. Canvassing and a marked register are essential activities and can make all the difference between victory and defeat in a marginal seat. The Labour Party's failure to organise the postal vote, which contrasts with Conservative efficiency in this respect, has often contributed to their candidate's defeat in a marginal constituency. So, obviously, an efficient local organisation has an important part to play.

Constituency parties come into their own, when the time arrives to select a Parliamentary candidate, although the NEC has the over-riding say and must approve the local choice. Transport House maintains an *A* list of trade union-sponsored candidates and a *B* list of individual members. Every aspirant must be nominated by a ward committee or affiliated organisation. The selection procedure is a solemn and awe-inspiring occasion. Potential candidates who have been short-listed are called in one by one before a special meeting of the GMC and must take a brief speech about themselves and their views, before submitting to a barrage of questions. No discussion is allowed about the merits or demerits of a candidate and votes are cast on the basis of one man, one vote, in a secret ballot. Sometimes the NEC can arrange the nomination of a candidate for whom it wants to find a seat, but, as in the Tory Party, local people are usually very jealous of their prerogative and resent the idea that somebody is being foisted on them.

Once a candidate has become an MP he is usually there for life – unless he breaks party rules to such an extent that he is expelled by the NEC. In poorer constituencies a candidate who has trade union backing, and consequently financial support, has a greater chance of being selected than an individual, who is not allowed to pay out of his own pocket towards constituency expenses.

Most local parties only come alive when elections are in the offing and, apart from the faithful few, tend to hibernate in between. In theory these periods provide an opportunity for building up the party and advancing political education. One of the recommendations of the Simpson report was that each party should appoint a political education officer, to arrange meetings and discussions, and to 'train' members in political activity. In practice the amount of time and energy devoted to such activities varies enormously. Some parties spend most of their time in social and fund-raising activities, arranging jumble sales, raffles, outings and tea parties, in the belief that new recruits are won through social contact and that politics are rather a bore to them. Most parties are so short of money that fund-raising is one of their main pre-occupations – gambling schemes generally produce about 50 per cent of their income and some local parties have grown very rich through football totes.

On the whole ward meetings tend to be dull and to get bogged down in business matters. The ward is not a natural unit of common interest – any more than is a geographical trade union branch. Attendance is usually low and limited to the party activists who turn up and vote each other into key positions and put forward militant resolutions for conference.

These activitists, the foot-sloggers, canvassers, envelope-addressers and tea-makers provide the backbone of the party. Without them the local constituency party would barely function. They regard themselves as the 'p b i' of the movement.

HEAD OFFICE

Party conference may be the 'fountain of authority' but Transport House provides the mechanism. This eight-storey rather uninspiring brick building in Smith Square has been the party headquarters since 1928 when Ernest Bevin invited the party and the TUC to share his new office. The TUC left in 1958 and the party is now looking for new quarters, as the giant Transport Union needs more elbow-room.

It is all very different from the early days when head office was housed in a 'dark and unsuitable' back room in Ramsay MacDonald's flat in Lincoln's Inn Fields at a rent of £25 per annum. A few years later it moved to a room in Ebury Street, but even there, as Beatrice Webb wrote in 1918, it was cramped and confined. 'The Labour Party is the most ramshackle institution in its topmost storey. Henderson sits alone in the untidy office' with a 'decrepit staff'.

Arthur Henderson combined the job of party secretary with being a Member of Parliament, and still retained it when he was foreign secretary in the second Labour Government. In spite of his frequent absences from the office on Parliamentary and other duties, he managed to dominate the party organisation. When he retired in 1932 the Executive decided that no future secretary should be allowed to become a Member of Parliament, but should concentrate on party administration.

The party secretary occupies a key position in the Labour movement. As administrator, he is in charge of running the machine and as a policy-maker he can exert influence within the National Executive Committee. Labour leaders do not relish the idea of having a strong man in Transport House and have resisted the idea, which has been widely canvassed at various times, that the party should adopt the Tory system and appoint a Director-General, with greater power and prestige, to manage the party. They feel that there are already enough prima donnas in the movement.

Henderson was succeeded by J. S. Middleton, an unobtrusive and uncontroversial figure, who had been acting secretary. He rarely intervened in political debates and played little part in policy making. Morgan Phillips, who succeeded him in 1944, was more in the Henderson mould, though without the opportunity to enter Parliament. A shrewd and ambitious Welshman, he carved a niche for himself in the international movement, becoming President of the Socialist International in 1951. He was furious when, on the NEC trip to China in the late 1950s, Nye Bevan reminded him: 'You're only the servant of the Executive,' for he saw himself as a spokesman and policy-maker.

Phillips managed to keep on good terms with all the factions of the NEC at a time of increasing personal tension, His closest associate was the wise and wily miners' leader, Sam Watson. He never got on with Herbert Morrison, who regarded party organisation as his own bailiwick and resented the fact that Phillips never consulted him. Despite a series of election defeats during the 1950s and the criticisms of party organisation contained in the Wilson report, Morgan Phillips remained imperturbable, immovable and influential.

Phillips retired through illness in 1961 and was succeeded by Len Williams, the national agent, a likeable, genial and unassuming party official. George Brown, as chairman of the NEC organisation sub committee, played an increasing part in internal party affairs. When Williams retired in 1968, it was widely expected that Tony Greenwood, who was believed to be Wilson's own choice, would be selected. Instead the NEC adopted Harry Nicholas, who had been Frank Cousins' number two in the TGWU and was regarded as more 'reliable' by the trade union group. Nicholas was approaching retiring age, so that his appointment was very much in the nature of a caretaker.

The choice of a successor to Harry Nicholas in 1972 produced a photo-finish in the contest between Ron Hayward, the national agent, and Gwyn Morgan, the assistant secretary. The NEC was split equally and Wedgwood Benn gave his casting vote to Hayward. Gwyn

Morgan was too much of a European and too close to Roy Jenkins for his liking.

Ron Hayward, hitherto an unknown figure outside party circles, was given more precise terms of reference than his predecessors had had, i.e. 'front-line' responsibility for ensuring that party conference decisions are carried out, direct access to the Leader, the Shadow Cabinet and the right to speak at Parliamentary party meetings. He made it plain that he intends to carry out these responsibilities. Hayward has a lifetime's experience of party work, having held various offices before becoming regional secretary of the sprawling southern region. He speaks with a broad Oxfordshire (not Oxford) accent, is genial, sometimes flippant in manner, leans to the left and upholds the sanctity of conference decisions.

The general secretary is in charge of seven departments at Transport House: the secretary's, organisation, women, international, research, information, and finance. The two departments which come into most contact with the outside world are research and information. When the party was in Government, there were frequent complaints that Transport House was being by-passed, since Ministers relied on their civil servants to brief them. In Opposition, the research department, headed by Terry Pitt, is kept busy providing MPs and ex-Ministers with facts and figures, as well as preparing policy documents for the NEC.

Public relations have long been the Achilles' heel of the Labour Party, which has never managed to project itself in the same way as the Conservative Party has done. The department, however, has been strengthened and enlarged and had its budget increased. A new Labour weekly was launched in 1971 under an independent editor, and, according to Percy Clark, head of the information department, was breaking even in mid-1972. The party still relies on the voluntary help and advice given by sympathetic journalists, broadcasters, and advertising people. Transport House officials, in general, have become more open and friendly in their dealings with the press, but their task has not been made easier by outbursts against newspapers, and television

D

such as that made by Wedgwood Benn at Blackpool in 1972.

From the election point of view, the organisation department, under the National agent (now Reg Underhill) is the most important in the Labour hierarchy. It is responsible for the entire party organisation within the country, including candidates, agents, local and Parliamentary elections, speakers and the regional machinery.

There are eleven regional offices, whose main function is to help build up parties in their areas and co-ordinate the activities of the various affiliated organisations. Regional councils hold annual conferences, on the same representational basis as the main party conference, but they are limited to the discussion of regional matters. The councils have pressed for greater powers, but the Simpson Committee ruled that there was no case for extending their scope. 'There cannot be more than one Labour Party determining national and international policy, and there should be no difficulty in finding subjects of regional importance to occupy usefully the time of regional annual meetings,' was its verdict.

The Labour Party recently set up a national agency service – yet another of the Simpson recommendations – but it only touches the fringe of the problem. Out of 141 full-time organisers, only 40 were employed centrally, the rest being appointed by local constituency parties.

The number of agents has been steadily declining. In 1951 there were 296, but on the eve of the 1970 election there were only 141 to cover 618 constituencies!

Of the 141 nearly half were employed in safe Labour seats and a third in marginal Labour constituencies. There were only eight agents per fifty-four constituencies in the West Midlands, 9 for 51 in Yorkshire and 7 for 71 in Scotland.

The present size of the agency force is clearly painfully inadequate to meet election needs and to build up local party activities between times. The most obvious solution would be to make head office, rather than individual constituency parties, responsible for their appointment and salaries, and thus provide them with job security and career prospects. Under effective central direction they could be deployed in the seats which the party has a chance of holding or winning. The agents, organised in the National Union of Labour Organisers, regard themselves as the Cinderellas of the party, being underpaid, overworked and lacking support and recognition.

FINANCE

Compared to the Conservatives, the Labour Party is poor, though it is sometimes said that the trade union contributions represent the equivalent of the businessmen's subvention of the Tories. Despite the unions' financial resources, the party, in common with most other organisations, has felt the effect of rising costs. In 1971, affiliation fees produced an income of £483,269, of which £422,865 came from the unions. Other sources of income brought the total to £570,581 compared with £516,110 in 1970. But soaring costs of administration, higher staff salaries and publishing expenses resulted in an excess of expenditure over income of about £100,000. To help meet the deficit affiliation fees are periodically raised. The rate, which was 1s a year (5p) in 1961 stood at 10p in 1972, rising to 12½p in 1973 and 15p in 1974. The subscription for individual members was also raised, to £1.20 a year, 10p a month.

The party has a substantial reserve fund, but this is regarded as only to be used in time of elections. When does an election campaign begin? Many commentators consider it short-sighted to hoard funds, when in fact a new election campaign might be said to begin on the day after polling day.

Increasing fees is the simplest method of raising revenue, but there is a limit to which this can be done, and it is not necessarily the best way of countering falling membership. Even so, party officials say that members are getting their party on the cheap.

The NEC is always coming out with new fund-raising schemes. In 1971 it introduced a development fund, towards which local parties were asked to contribute 10 per cent of their 1972 income. Another scheme was for a motor insurance scheme – but this was overwhelmingly rejected at the conference. Various fund-raising projects, such as the Golden Prize clubs scheme, the 'Fighting fivers' campaign and a Salvation-Army type appeal were launched but met with little success. The NEC appointed a financial expert, Oliver Stutchbury, as financial adviser in 1966, but after four 'frustrating years' he resigned in 1970, commenting that 'financially and organisationally the party is in a critically unhappy position'. In his resignation letter he said: 'My job as the party's fund raising adviser cannot be performed effectively in the present state of the party's organisation in the country. I have resisted the impulse to resign before on the assurance that a high level inquiry was to be instituted at the 1970 conference. No inquiry has been forthcoming, and I can see no point whatever in my carrying on.'

This was not exactly a happy start for the party's plans to retrieve its fortunes.

What then can be done? One ingenious scheme put forward by Dick Leonard MP at a Fabian New Year school in January 1973 is that Britain should consider adopting the system whereby political parties in West Germany, Finland and Sweden receive public subsidies. 'If it is not accepted as a public responsibility to finance political parties, Labour will become even more financially dependent upon the trade unions than in the past and the Conservatives will be even more in the pay of big business.

V

Trade unions and the party

There is a popular conception that the trade unions are run by a handful of big bosses and that the Labour Party slavishly obeys the crack of their whip. Another, rather different, theory is that, with the erosion of the class nature of British society, more workers come to identify themselves with the middle class and the old party loyalties are loosened. This was almost certainly an element in the 1959 defeat, when the Macmillan slogan 'You've never had it so good' appealed to the more highly-paid and skilled workers who were buying their own homes and cars, and appeared to be fulfilling the Tory image of a 'property-owning democracy'.

In the early 1960s many writers pointed out that the departure of the TUC from Transport House to Bloomsbury involved more than a physical separation. There was a psychological significance in the splitting-up of headquarters, and the question was increasingly asked: Will the trade unions become exclusively concerned with industrial, rather than political, affairs and be more like the American unions which are not wedded to their own specific party philosophy?

Martin Harrison, in his study *Trade Unions and the Labour Party after 1945*[1] wrote: 'The long-term trend is for the unions' part in the life of the Labour Party to slacken ... the unions' hopes from Labour are less and less directly and immediately related to their industrial needs.' Harrison however concluded: 'The unions' continued withdrawal from participation would leave the movement like an ageing elm.

[1] M. Harrison, *Trade Unions and the Labour Party after 1945* (Allen & Unwin 1960).

Though outwardly it might be sound, its heart would be dead.'

The alliance between the Labour Party and the unions was formed in 1900 at the Memorial Hall, Faringdon Street. The party was in fact the child of the TUC which the year before had decided to embark on political action. Its immediate objectives were limited. They were 'to ensure that working-class opinion should be represented in the House of Commons by men sympathetic with the aims and demands of the Labour movement and whose candidatures are promoted by one or other of the organised movements'. No mention here about the need to win power or formulate policies, no mention of socialist objectives. Indeed, early moves to commit the party to definite policies designed to overthrow capitalism were rejected, as were proposals to bind the party to accept all proposals emanating from the TUC.

The party developed as a broad and loosely-knit federation of trade unions and socialist societies, without very much sense of direction. George Wardle, chairman of the National Executive Committee and a Minister in the Lloyd George coalition, said in 1917: 'From the very first the ties which bound the party together were of the loosest possible kind. It has steadily, and in my opinion wisely, always declined to be bound by any programme, to subscribe to any dogma or to lay down any creed . . . Its strength has been its catholicity, its tolerance, its welcoming of all shades of political and even revolutionary thought, providing that its chief object – the unifying of the workers' political power – was not damaged or hindered thereby.'

A year later, Arthur Henderson's Constitution defined the role and composition of the party in a dogmatic and detailed form, which contradicted Wardle's thesis, while Sidney Webb's statement – 'Labour and the new social order' – laid down the broad basis of future policy. Nevertheless, even if the Labour Party has at times seemed to ignore the elements of tolerance and latitude, it has remained a broad coalition of varying, and often conflicting interests.

Throughout its history, the party has been associated with the trade unions. As shown in the previous chapter, they are the dominant element, in terms of money and votes. They provide about 85 to 90 per cent of the party's finance and at election times can be relied upon to make massive contributions to campaign funds. They effectively decide the composition of the National Executive Committee and carry five-sixths of the voting power at party conference with their block votes.

The block vote has long been a subject of contention and controversy. There is nothing in the party Constitution about it, nor is there any bar, in theory, to the splitting of a delegation vote. In practice this is rarely, if ever, done. The defenders of the system argue that it is a traditional trade union practice and that there is no viable alternative. It used to be regarded as a brake on the extremists in the constituency parties. Thus Sidney Webb once said that 'the constituency parties were frequently unrepresentative groups of nonentities dominated by fanatics and cranks, and extremists, and that *if* the block vote of the trade unions were eliminated it would be impracticable to continue to vest the control of policy in Labour Party conferences'.[1]

Its critics maintain that it is undemocratic and unfair that one man should hold up a card committing the entire affiliated membership of his union to a policy upon which the rank and file have not been consulted. In some cases a union conference may have laid down policy, but often an issue arises afterwards – some unions only hold conferences every other year – and a snap decision has to be taken.

Attlee hit the nail on the head when he wrote: 'The main objection is generally less against the method of voting than against the results of voting. Those who make the loudest song about the block vote are significantly silent when it happens to be cast with their own views.'[2]

Attlee's point was vividly illustrated in the late 1950s when Aneurin Bevan won the Treasurership. Bevan had stood unsuccessfully for many years running against Hugh Gaitskell, but in 1956 he beat George Brown by a narrow margin, thanks to the last minute decision of USDAW to

[1] Beatrice Webb's Diaries, 1930, quoted in R. McKenzie, *British political parties* (Heinemann Education, 1953).
[2] *Labour Party in Perspective* (Gollancz 1949).

back him. Nye Bevan had once described the block vote as 'a travesty of democracy'. When I asked him at a hastily-called press conference afterwards 'What do you think of the block vote now, Nye?' he chuckled and said 'It's OK when it goes your way.'

Since the capture of the conference by the left-wing unions, little has been heard about the block vote from the groups which used to complain most vociferously about it. It is the right-wing and moderate elements which would seem to have cause for complaint.

If all trade union delegations voted the same way they would swamp the conference. In practice there is no automatic trade union alignment. Apart from issues such as the Industrial Relations Act, on which there is unanimity, unions may be sharply divided on policies.

Up to the mid-fifties, the Transport Workers, Miners and General and Municipal Workers formed a powerful triple alliance, which regularly supported right-wing resolutions. Their respective leaders, Arthur Deakin, Will Lawther and Tom Williamson were a triumvirate which would tolerate neither rebels nor minorities, and was dedicated to the pursuit of smashing Bevan. They were joined by a fourth man, Lincoln Evans, of the steel-workers, who made up in astuteness what he lacked in voting power. Their combined vote was consistently cast in favour of right-wing policies. For example, they gained a narrow victory for the leadership over German rearmament in 1954, even though the engineers, railwaymen and shop-workers voted against.

It was about this time that Barbara Castle cried out in anguish: 'The Labour movement is in danger of dying a death of 3 million cuts – the block votes of four men.'

The four men invariably supported right-wing 'safe' candidates for election to the National Executive Committee. Their move to make Herbert Morrison run against Arthur Greenwood for Treasurer in 1953 failed – because Morrison, as they put it, 'ran away' at the last minute. But usually the big bosses were able to get their nominees elected, and often suggested to them that unless they voted a certain way support might be withheld. Eirene White was an early victim of the practice. She decided to withdraw her candidature for the Women's section because she said: 'I have good reason to think that the leaders of some of the larger unions have decided that a person of my moderate views is not acceptable to them.' She could not hold a middle-of-the-road course between 'the bludgeons of the right and poisoned arrows of the left'.

The element of horse-trading in NEC elections was one of the least attractive features of the Labour Party in those days – happily the practice has declined.

The situation changed suddenly and dramatically with the advent of Frank Cousins as leader of the Transport Workers Union.

Cousins, an ex-lorry driver from Yorkshire and hitherto a little-known official in the union, had been catapulted to the top after the deaths of Deakin and his immediate successor, Jock Tiffin, six months later. Stubbornly and uncompromisingly socialist in his views, he broke the right-wing barrier with his one speech against wage restraint at the Blackpool TUC in 1956. This changed the course of the entire movement, introducing a random element in place of the old inflexibility. 'You never know what Frank will do next,' his colleagues used to complain, and the prime concern of many of them was to 'contain' Cousins, for they knew they could not muzzle him.

The old-guard, right-wing alliance was shattered. In any case, Lawther had retired, Evans had gone to the Steel Board, and Tom Williamson could not hold the fort on his own. Also shattered was the doctrine advanced by Vincent Tewson, then general secretary, after Labour's defeat in the 1951 election. He gave an assurance that the TUC would seek to work 'amicably' with the new Conservative Government – an assurance that makes strange reading in 1973.

The Tewson theory worked for a time, so long as the conciliatory Sir Walter Monckton was at the Ministry of Labour. Relations were so cordial that one leading member of the General Council once told me: 'At all costs we mustn't bugger Monckton.' The policy of amicable co-operation wore a bit thin when Iain Macleod, the new Minister of Labour, took a tougher line and became involved in a head-on clash with Frank Cousins over the London bus strike. The TUC, which had started by blessing the busmen's cause, refused to support Cousins' move to spread the strike and risk direct confrontation with the Government. The General Council continued its broad policy of co-operation with the Government and sought to avoid getting too closely and publicity identified with the Labour Party. Hugh Gaitskell's sudden arrival at the Blackpool congress, on the eve of the 1959 election, while enthusiastically welcomed by most of the delegates, was frowned on by many of the leaders. They regarded the incursion of an emotional, electioneering speech as an embarrassment.

The General Council is always sensitive to the feelings of its non-political unions. These represent an influential and growing body within the TUC. Local government officers, teachers and several civil service unions have no party affiliation. Congress agenda often carries a resolution declaring support for the Labour Party. Customarily, the non-political unions abstain or discreetly absent themselves when the vote is taken. But in 1957 their dilemma was brought into the open by Emrys Thomas, of the Ministry of Labour staff association. Speaking on behalf of other civil service unions, as well as his own, he asked that their abstention should be recorded on a TGWU resolution on wages which ended by calling for a return of the Labour Government. 'These unions which are loyal to the TUC are obliged not to ally themselves with any political party; indeed we have always regarded the TUC itself as an industrial instrument and not tied to a political party,' he said, amid loud cries of 'Shame'.

The same considerations apply to many unions which represent professional workers, and are affiliated to the TUC but not to the party, such as journalists, bank employees, medical practitioners, airline pilots and certain professional engineering and scientific organisations.

The decline in employment in traditional labour strongholds, such as mines, railways and shipyards, has to some extent been offset by the growth of unionism among white-collar workers. Clerks, typists, managers and supervisors do not automatically subscribe to socialism in the same way as miners and railwaymen, whose roots lie deep in the Labour Party. But it is surely significant that in the voting strength at party conference (1972) Clive Jenkins' meteorically growing Association of Scientific, Managerial and Technical Staffs came tenth in voting strength, after the National Union of Railwaymen, and the Clerical and Administrative Workers were twelfth, ahead of the steel workers.

It is perhaps necessary to stress that the TUC General Council cannot dictate to its affiliated unions and that, contrary to a widely held fallacy, the TUC as such has no political connections. Affiliation to the Labour Party is entirely a matter for individual unions, as is the way in which they operate their political funds. The question of contracting-out versus contracting-in to a union's political fund has long been a source of argument between the Conservatives and the Labour Party. After the Attlee Government repealed the Conservatives 1927 Act (which had provided for contracting-in) there was a dramatic increase in the numbers paying the political levy, from 2,917,000 to 5,613,000 – or about double. Joseph Goldstein, in his study of the Transport Workers Union[1] said 'this fantastic increase is startling but considerable evidence of apathy'. Sir Hartley Shawcross, on the other hand thought it was evidence that no one was being compelled to contribute to political funds against his will. Among some unions, for example the miners, there is virtually no contracting-out; in others, particularly those catering for white-collar workers, the rate is fairly high.

The question of how far trade unionists take part in political activity is too complex to be dealt with in this chapter. It has been admirably surveyed by Martin Harrison, though there is scope for bringing his 1960 study up to date. All that can be said, briefly, is that, as with local Labour Party branches, it is only a minority of activists who play a part in political or trade union decision making. The vast majority are apathetic.

At the top the unions tend to send their number twos to serve on the National Executive Committee. Their general

[1] J. Goldstein, *The Government of British Trade Unions* (Allen & Unwin 1950).

secretaries regard it as more important and more prestigious to be elected to the TUC General Council.

During the late 1960s the trade union movement began to swing violently to the left, as far to the left as it had been to the right in the 1950s. Jack Jones, at the Transport Union, carried on the Cousins tradition. Jones, if anything further to the left than Cousins and certainly more consistent and clear-headed in his advocacy of left-wing policies, continued to build up his union's strength. Son of a Liverpool docker, and himself a former dock-worker, he was born into the Labour movement. He fought with the International Brigade in Spain and was Midlands organiser for the TGWU at a time when the car workers were becoming increasingly militant. He joined the board of the weekly Tribune and writes, as he talks, pungently, though without malice. He is a formidable negotiator who knows just how far a door can be pushed open. He is also an efficient administrator, and under his guidance the union mounted effective campaigns on behalf of lower-paid workers and old-age pensioners.

The TGWU has been in the left-wing camp since 1956, so there was nothing new when Jones took over from Cousins in 1968. But that same year a stunning change in the balance of power occurred when Hugh Scanlon was elected President of the Amalgamated Union of Engineering Workers, (AUEW), beating John Boyd, the moderate Salvationist member of the AEU Executive who had been Bill Carron's 'favourite son'.

Carron had frequently delivered the AEU vote into the Gaitskell camp and managed to control his militant left-wingers by a mixture of guile and toughness. On many occasions he cast the union's vote according to the way he interpreted the union's policy, which did not always coincide with the views of his delegation. There were usually angry protests, but 'Carron's Law' became a recognised feature of TUC and party conferences. Scanlon, a one-time shop steward convenor in Manchester and an ex-Communist, is completely unswerving, unsubtle and die-hard in his socialism, scorning manoeuvre and compromise. His philosophy is that the unions' rôle 'must be to change society itself, not merely to get the best out of existing society'. He stood out for a boycott of the Industrial Relations Act machinery – at a cost of heavy fines for his union – and for complete opposition to the Common Market, and to talks with the Tory Government on incomes policy.

Another significant change at the top was the retirement of George Woodcock in 1969 and his succession by Vic Feather. Woodcock always regarded himself and the TUC as apolitical and had a barely concealed contempt for some party politicians. He approached problems from an intellectual, rather than an emotional, angle and liked to argue matters as he went along, judging issues on their merits, irrespective of whence they came. He rarely took part in election activities.

Vic Feather provides a complete contrast. He is genial, extrovert, with a down-to-earth Yorkshire directness and humour. As his full name, Victor Grayson Hardie Feather, suggests, he is a committed and convinced Labour man. He flings himself into election campaigns with great fervour, and is unstinting of his time and energy (he even came to speak for me in Petersfield in 1964!) But he is first and foremost a trade unionist. If any Labour politicians were to make demands which he thought incompatible with trade union interests, he would always put his union loyalties first. This was shown in the conflict which arose over the Labour Government's proposed industrial relations legislation 'In place of strife'. As related in an earlier chapter, the toughness of Feather and his associates and the groundswell of trade union opinion, forced Wilson to climb down.

When the Heath Government introduced its own plans to deal with the unions and curb strikes, the full fury of the trade union movement was unleashed. This, they said, was Government interference in free collective bargaining and the introduction of the Law into industrial relations was in complete contradiction to the Donovan Royal Commission which had upheld the principle of voluntary negotiation and dismissed the idea of legal sanctions.

Even before the terms of the Industrial Relations Bill were known Jack Jones told the Labour Party conference in 1970: 'The proposed Tory legislation will create ill-will and suspicion and what is needed is goodwill and good faith. If industrial relations become based on threats of legal action, sensible people on both sides of industry know that it just will not work.' A year later, when the Bill was on the Statute book, he called on the next Labour Government to repeal it immediately and to pledge no interference in free negotiations. 'This Act, if rigidly applied, will put back the clock 100 years ... It will be used to try to hold back our advance and threaten the very existence of free trade unionism.'

'This Act,' said Eric Heffer MP, 'is the most pernicious and vicious piece of class legislation that has come before this country since before the Second World War.'

Pressure inside and outside Parliament failed to halt the passage of the Bill, which duly became law in the summer of 1971. The TUC decided to adopt a policy of non-co-operation. This meant boycotting all the bodies set up under the Act, including the National Industrial Relations Court, the Commission on Industrial Relations and the industrial tribunals – although it was agreed that unions should have the right to defend themselves before such bodies. Affiliated unions which refused to de-register in accordance with TUC policy were suspended by Congress in 1972 and by the end of the year some thirty unions, mainly smaller and white-collar workers' organisations, had been recommended for expulsion.

The Act certainly did not succeed in its objective of limiting strikes, or promoting industrial harmony. More days were lost through stoppages in 1972 than in any year since the General Strike year of 1926. Most of the days were lost in two big battles, involving miners and dockers, and in guerilla-type activities by engineers and building workers. The events leading up to the jailing of five dockers for contempt of Court, and the inept handling of the railwaymen's ballot tended to bring the whole paraphernalia of the Act into disrepute. It had, as Wilson said in the Parliamentary debate in July 1971, 'led to total confusion and unnecessary division and bitterness in industrial relations'. Reg Prentice, Shadow Minister of Employment, and many other MPs counselled that, bad as the Law might be, it must be observed.

The Labour Party pledged itself to repeal the Act as soon as it was returned to office but there was general agreement on the need to put something in its place to deal with industrial relations. During the winter of 1972–3, Labour and union leaders worked out a formula for legislation to replace the Act. The whole approach would be to keep the Law out of industrial relations and collective bargaining, and develop along the lines of the Donovan Report. 'In place of strife' was finally buried. Among measures foreshadowed in 'Programme for Britain' were statutory protection for unions and the right to exercise their functions, a new non-Government agency for conciliation and arbitration, and the promotion of industrial democracy and workers' participation.

The story of the Conservative Government's anti-inflation legislation, with its statutory control over wages and manufacturers' prices, is a continuing one. It had the effect of drawing the unions and the party even more closely together in their opposition to the Government. The outline of an economic strategy to curb inflation was prepared and a joint statement issued at the end of January. Of this, the *Guardian* commented: 'The Labour Party and the TUC plighted their troth – and Congress House wore the trousers in no uncertain manner.' Mr Wilson described the statement as 'one of the biggest steps we have ever taken in working out a policy together'. Its main stresses were on the need to control prices, particularly food prices, with proposals for public ownership of land, increased subsidies for transport and higher pensions. On the crucial issue of wages and incomes the statement was evasive, confining itself to the rejection of statutory control. The 'great compact' was publicly solemnised at a joint Wilson/Feather conference at the end of February.

The Government, not unnaturally, rubbed in the point that the Labour Party was 'pandering' to the trade unions. Lord Carrington, Conservative Party chairman, said that the so-called agreement made the Labour Party 'into little more than the parliamentary mouthpiece of the militants'. The inherent danger in this situation was noted by Anthony Crosland *(The Observer*, 31 January 1973): 'If we are thought, as we sometimes are, to be the creature of the unions and exclusively identified with them, then Mr Heath could occupy Number Ten for a long, long time.'

In the same article, however, he pointed to the example of Senator McGovern's disastrous defeat in the US Presidential election, largely because he had neglected the Democrats' traditional trade union support and concentrated on policies which appealed, in the main, to middle-class interests. By the same token one of the reasons why Labour lost in 1970 was its failure to attract trade union votes.

The problem of the relations between the political and industrial wings of the movement has been with Labour ever since its foundation. There are bound to be divergencies of interest, as Attlee observed as long ago as 1937: 'It is inevitable that there should from time to time be misunderstandings between the industrial and the political sides of the movement.' Vic Feather summed up the position in 1969 when he said: 'The Labour Party and the trade union movement each has its own responsibilities and neither side wants to strain the loyalties which exist. If you look round the world to see where social democracy is strongest, you will find a strong united trade union movement and a strong united social democratic party – and the two have a close understanding.'

A recognition of this situation would seem to offer the best hope of satisfactory mutual relationships in the future.

The essential need is that the politicians must recognise that the British unions are deeply committed to the voluntary principle of free collective bargaining. Otherwise the tensions that developed in 1969–70 will never be lowered.

VI

Labour MPs

The Parliamentary Labour Party, like the national party, represents a coalition of widely differing interests, ranging from the far left to the far right. It was estimated that the Opposition after 1970 contained roughly equal numbers of the Tribune group and the so-called Jenkinsites – each commanding about seventy supporters. Most Labour MPs form a solid block in the centre and the fact that they vote unerringly as the Whips dictate has earned them the title of 'lobby fodder'. Iain Macleod, less kindly and less accurately, once referred to the centre as the 'blancmange' of the party. Colourless some of the Members may be, but they certainly don't wobble! Few back-bench MPs have the same opportunities of appearing on TV or such radio programmes as 'The World at One', or of writing articles for the weekly press which are open to the more controversial and colourful Members. There is thus an inevitable undercurrent of resentment among the majority. Arthur Deakin in the 1950s referred to the Bevanites as 'a group of frustrated journalists', a hyperbole which, though to a lesser extent, still reflects the atmosphere in the 1970s, and never more so than over the sixty-nine MPs who defied the Party Whip over Europe in October 1971 and thereby 'kept Heath in power'.

The relations between the PLP and party conference are dealt with in Chapter VIII. A brief description about the way the PLP functions, and its responsibilities, may here be appropriate.

The Parliamentary Labour Party comprises all elected Members who accept the party constitution and the party Whip. It was formed in 1906, superseding the original Labour Representation Committee which lacked cohesion and of whose members it was said 'Each was a party in

E

himself'. When the number of Labour Members rose to twenty-nine in the 1906 election it became necessary to introduce some order and method into its proceedings, and at its very first meeting, on 12 February, Arthur Henderson reported: 'We can congratulate ourselves today that a real live independent Labour Party, having its own chairman, its own deputy chairman and its own whips, is now an accomplished fact in British politics.'

The rôle and importance of the PLP vary according to whether Labour is in Government or Opposition. In Opposition there are fewer restraints and ex-Ministers mingle freely with ordinary MPS in the tea-bar and lobbies of the House. In Government, on the other hand, Ministers are usually so overworked and so cocooned in their departments, that they have little time to keep in touch with rank and file opinion, inside or outside the House. This was a sore point under the Attlee administration. Wilfred Fienburgh, then research secretary at Transport House, wrote: 'Ministers, heavily immersed in day-to-day governmental responsibilities, assumed what amounted to a power of veto in the framing of election manifestos. This, plus ministerial caution, ministerial fatigue and ministerial remoteness, resulted in the strangled and emasculated manifestos of 1950 and 1951.'

Ministers tend to look on back-bench MPS purely as 'lobby fodder' or, if they show signs of independence, as unmitigated nuisances. On their side, many back-bench MPS, unless they are junior Ministers or Parliamentary private secretaries, become increasingly frustrated at having to defend policies with which they do not agree and cannot influence, while their status is reduced to that of welfare officers for their constituents.

The same gap, the same overloading and fatigue of Ministers, was just as pronounced under the Wilson Government.

When he was Leader of the House in 1945, Herbert Morrison, a wise Parliamentarian, set up a small liaison committee to keep the Government in touch with its supporters in the House. In theory this committee provided Ministers with a useful means of keeping themselves informed about the state of party morale and enabled them to nip incipient revolts in the bud. There are, of course, other sources of information. The Whips keep their ears to the ground and so do the Parliamentary private secretaries. For all his aloofness, Attlee was kept well informed by his PPS Arthur Moyle. But the system of communications did not always work so well in practice as it did on paper.

After 1945, a new system of allocating MPs to subject and area groups was introduced. This had existed before, but on a rather haphazard basis. MPs now belong to area groups, corresponding to the regions of the Labour Party organisation, and serve on subject groups, dealing with a variety of issues ranging from farming to finance. The most influential is the trade union group, which as related on page 29, was instrumental in defeating Barbara Castle's 'In place of strife' policy, and played a crucial part in the debates over the Heath Government's Industrial Relations Bill. It is composed of MPs whose candidature has been sponsored by a union, even though they may not themselves be of working-class origin.

Indeed, a remarkable feature of the modern Labour Party in the House is the extent to which traditional trade union MPs have been overtaken by professional people. The process started in 1945 when the great flood of new MPs, many of them straight from the forces, included many middle-class and professional men and women. Trade union-sponsored members dropped to less than one-third of the total and the proportion of working people, selected as candidates or elected as MPs, has continued to decline. In 1970 more than half the total number of Labour candidates were from the professions, and the number of university graduates increased markedly.[1]

The list of elected candidates in 1970 was headed by teachers (56), barristers (34), and journalists (27). There were only 22 miners, 33 skilled and 17 semi-skilled workers.

The changing composition of the PLP between 1951 and 1970 is shown in tabular form:

[1] See D. E. Butler and M. Pinto-Duschinsky, *The British General Election of 1970* (Macmillan 1971).

	Per cent		
	1951	*1966*	*1970*
Professional	35	43	40
Business	9	9	10
Miscellaneous white collar	19	18	16
Workers	37	30	26
Elementary education	26	22	21
Secondary	54	60	62
Public school	20	18	17
University	41	51	53

The Parliamentary Labour Party comes under the direction of the Parliamentary Committee, known as the 'Shadow Cabinet' when the party is in Opposition. The Committee consists of the leader, deputy leader, PLP chairman and deputy chairman, the chief Whip and the chairman of the Labour group in the House of Lords and its chief Whip. All are *ex-officio* members and the Commons officers are subject to annual election. (The Leader is not subject to re-election when he is Prime Minister.) The whole party in the House elects twelve representatives and the Peers elect one. Up to 1924 MPs were expected to choose from a tally of all the Members in the House, but the list was later reduced to more manageable proportions.
places.

In 1972, there were thirty-one candidates for the twelve places. The results were:

1	Reg Prentice ⎱	154	(13)
	Shirley Williams ⎰		(3)
3	Anthony Crosland	148	(8)
4	Michael Foot	146	(2)
5	James Callaghan	142	(4)
6	Denis Healey	137	(12)
7	William Ross	134	(5)
8	Fred Peart	128	(6)
9	Harold Lever	125	(7)
10	Merlyn Rees	107	(25)
11	Anthony Wedgwood Benn	106	(10)
12	Peter Shore ⎱	102	(11)
	John Silkin ⎰		(14)

(Previous year's placing in brackets)
John Silkin stood down in favour of Peter Shore.

The voting results produced a healthy balance between moderate and left-wing opinion, at a time when the National Executive Committee and the trade unions were swinging rapidly to the left.

The spectacular rise of Merlyn Rees from twenty-fifth place to tenth and of Reg Prentice from thirteenth to first show how much a man's reputation can be made during a single Parliamentary session – Rees's over Northern Ireland, and Prentice's over the Industrial Relations Bill. Equally, Barbara Castle came fifteenth and her defeat was due to the long memories of trade union MPs who had never forgiven her for 'In place of strife'.

Two enthusiastic Europeans, Shirley Williams and Harold Lever, were counterbalanced by two equally enthusiastic anti-Marketeers, Michael Foot and Peter Shore.

The Times and most other newspapers praised the MPs for the good sense they had shown in picking their Committee. *Tribune*, however, was furious and claimed that there had been definite 'plumping' for right-wing candidates by 'a skilfully organised and determined campaign on the part of those in the PLP who have in the past been members of the right-wing Campaign for Democratic Socialism ... There is nothing sinister or unconstitutional about "plumping" but it should be noted that it was done by the CDS grouping to build up a coalition of forces which would apparently work together to defy conference decisions.' Incidentally it was the 'skilfully organised and determined campaign' and plumping by the Tribune group which secured the election of six Bevanites to the National Executive in 1952 and the defeat of Morrison and Dalton.

Five of the present Shadow Cabinet, excluding the *ex-officio* leader and deputy leader, are also members of the party National Executive. This overlapping of membership has long been a feature of the party. In theory it should make for smooth relations and mutual understanding. After 1972, with the left dominating the Executive and the right ahead in the Parliamentary committee, there was more risk of friction.

Voting for the National Executive Committee in October 1972 produced a clean sweep for the left in the constituency section, with the exception of Denis Healey who narrowly defeated Tom Driberg. Driberg had been the first swallow of the Bevanite summer and had been a member of the NEC for over twenty years.

The results were:
(Previous year's placing in brackets)

Michael Foot (–)	554,000
Wedgwood Benn (2)	399,000
Frank Allaun (5)	395,000
Barbara Castle (3)	359,000
Ian Mikardo (1)	346,000
Jean Lestor (4)	340,000
Denis Healey (6)	290,000

In the women's section elected by the whole conference, the results were equally spectacular. With the exception of Shirley Williams, all the women elected were anti-European and identified with the left. Eirene White lost her place.

Judith Hart (2)	4,703,000
Lena Jeger (3)	4,534,000
Renee Short (4)	4,032,000
Shirley Williams (5)	3,612,000
Joan Maynard (6)	2,974,000

In the contest for the Treasurership, James Callaghan secured 3,575,000 votes against his left-wing challenger Norman Atkinson's 2,624,000.

Thus in 1972–3, eleven out of twelve members of the NEC elected in the constituency and women's section were Members of Parliament, and of these all but two were on the left wing of the party.

The most important function of the PLP is to elect the party leader, and therefore potential Prime Minister. There is usually a contest for this key job, since ambitious MPs regard it as essential to keep their names on the list as potential leaders. Voting is by ballot. Once elected it is rare for a leader to be dislodged. The position of the party leader is examined in the next chapter.

VII

Labour leaders

The position of party leader is of comparatively recent origin in the history of the Labour movement. There is no reference to it in the 1918 Constitution, and up to 1922 the term 'Chairman' was exclusively used. But that year Ramsay MacDonald was elected "chairman *and leader*".

Since 1922 the Labour Party has had six leaders: MacDonald, 1922–31; Arthur Henderson, 1931–2; George Lansbury, 1932–5; Clement Attlee, 1935–55; Hugh Gaitskell, 1955–63; Harold Wilson, 1963– . Three of these – MacDonald, Attlee and Wilson – became Prime Minister.

Henderson and Lansbury were leaders at a time when the party was in a state of collapse. All the other four men exercised great authority and personal ascendancy. Each leader has adopted different styles and strategies, learning from the experience and mistakes of his predecessors. Thus Wilson has told us that he based himself in the conduct of Cabinet business on Attlee.

What are the qualities required of a Labour leader? What kind of personal characteristics make him acceptable to Members of Parliament and the movement outside? The best way to answer these questions is to look at the records and personalities of the men who have held this office.

The name of James Ramsay MacDonald is still anathema to most Labour people, especially among the older generation who remember personally how he deserted the party in 1931. There have been some recent attempts to rehabilitate him and to recall his lifetime of service to the movement up to 1931. He had been secretary of the party from 1900 to 1911, when he became chairman, resigning as a conscientious objector in the 1914–18 War. Even then he was a dominating figure. Beatrice Webb wrote in 1914 that he 'rules absolutely and the other Labour members stick to him as their only salvation from confusion'. Defeated in the Lloyd-George Khaki election landslide he returned to Parliament in 1922.

It was not altogether a surprise when that year he defeated J. R. Clynes who had proved an efficient but colourless chairman. MacDonald had retained his old ILP Clydeside reputation and his opposition to the 'imperialist' War won him much support in the party. His victory was helped by his active canvassing on his own behalf and by what Clynes later called 'complicated plans and schemes' for his defeat. Once elected MacDonald made it plain to all that he intended to be a leader in every sense of the word.

Then in his mid-fifties he was still extremely handsome with a resonant voice and an impressive platform manner. He seems to have had a measure of that elusive quality of charisma and certainly inspired great loyalty and admiration among party workers in the early days of his leadership. His relations with his immediate colleagues were not happy and he took little trouble to hide his contempt for them. He particularly disliked Henderson whom he tried to keep out of office when he was forming his first Cabinet. The distrust was probably mutual. Philip Snowden wrote in his autobiography: 'I had seen a good deal of him when he was chairman before the War and his passion for intrigue and compromise and his desire to be regarded as a "gentleman" by the other parties disqualified him to lead a party which contained so many members who had come into the House of Commons filled with enthusiasm for a fight.' Snowden regarded MacDonald's leftism as hypocrisy.

In January 1924 King George V asked MacDonald to form a Government. Harold Nicolson[1] recorded the King's diary note on the interview: 'I had an hour's talk with him; he impressed me very much. He wishes to do the right thing. Today twenty-five years ago dear Grandmama died. I wonder what she would have thought of a Labour Government!'

According to Nicolson, MacDonald was 'flattered and

[1] Harold Nicolson, *King George V* (Constable 1952).

even dazzled by His Majesty's forthright friendliness'. MacDonald was not the only Labour leader to be 'flattered and dazzled' by the reception at Buckingham Palace. Clynes wrote after the King had received members of the new Cabinet: 'I could not help marvelling at the strange turn of Fortune's wheel which had brought MacDonald, the starvelling clerk, Thomas the engine Driver, Henderson the foundry labourer and Clynes the mill-hand to this pinnacle beside the man whose forebears had been Kings for so many splendid generations.'

No wonder Republicanism has never made much headway in the British working class!

Both Henderson and Snowden resented the way in which MacDonald picked his 1924 Cabinet without consulting them, and there was general dissatisfaction at the small number of trade unionists appointed and at the choice of a Liberal peer and two Conservative peers to fill the positions of Lord President, Lord Chancellor and First Lord of the Admiralty. MacDonald, in Pooh Bah style combined the rôles of Prime Minister and Foreign Secretary, as well as being chairman of the NEC and party Treasurer. Beatrice Webb wrote in her diary that Sidney, then President of the Board of Trade, thought that 'JRM is head and and shoulders above the rest of the Cabinet'. A few weeks later she noted that he seemed to have become 'more aloof and autocratic towards his Ministers'.

The first Labour Government was elected on a minority vote. Labour won 191 seats, compared with the Conservatives' 258 and the Liberals' 158 – the ILP won 39 seats. It was thus dependent on Liberal support and was unable, or unwilling, to implement the policies laid down in 'Labour and the new social order', the joint Henderson-Webb statement of 1918 which remained the declaration of basic party principles for many years. The only progressive measure adopted was the Housing Act brought in by Clydesider John Wheatley, the only real left-winger in the Cabinet. As it was, the Government lasted for less than a year. The J. R. Campbell sedition case and the decision not to prosecute resulted in a combined Tory-Liberal majority which forced MacDonald to resign. The Zinoviev letter issue, a blatant piece of Tory scaremongering during the campaign, had its impact on an electorate which was not so sophisticated as that of today.

Troubles were not over for McDonald when he became leader of the Opposition. He faced mounting criticism from the ILP and from Lansbury and members of the National Executive. He had alienated large numbers of his colleagues and Labour supporters in the country by his arrogance and his failure to consult, or keep in touch with, the Labour movement outside Parliament.

MacDonald incurred the hostility of Citrine and Bevin, and of most leaders of the TUC, over his attitude towards the General Strike of 1926. During the Strike, the Parliamentary party had sat on the side-lines making appropriate noises – it was after all a trade union struggle – and when it was over MacDonald wrote. 'The General Strike is a weapon that cannot be wielded for industrial purposes. It is clumsy and ineffectual ... I hope that the result will be a thorough reconsideration of trade union tactics.'

Bevin[1] retorted: 'I cannot see my way clear to support the Labour Party and to take part in its propaganda so long as Mr J. R. MacDonald as its leader continues his present policy in relation to the industrial side.'

Arthur Henderson poured oil on the troubled waters, but there was never any reconciliation between Bevin and MacDonald.

In the 1929 election, Labour secured the largest number of seats and, though it still did not have a clear majority, agreed to form the Government. MacDonald's Cabinet was the mixture as before, though he dropped left-winger Wheatley and brought in George Lansbury to preside over the Office of Works. (Lansbury's 'Lido' in Hyde Park remains his permanent memorial.)

The second Labour administration was to prove an unmitigated disaster. As in 1924 MacDonald was engrossed in world affairs, although Henderson was actually Foreign Minister. He knew little about economics, and it is doubtful if he even played with matchsticks. Snowden, his Chancellor,

[1] See Alan Bullock, *The Life and Times of Ernest Bevin*, Vol. I (Heinemann 1960).

was putty in the hands of the Treasury and Bank of England officials. The chill wind of economic crisis blew across the Atlantic and at home unemployment was rising at an alarming rate. The party had given an election pledge 'to deal immediately and practically with this problem', but the total number of unemployed rose from just over 1 million when it took office in June 1929 to $2\frac{1}{2}$ million in December the following year, and to $2\frac{3}{4}$ million in July 1931.

There was growing revolt within the party. Oswald Mosley, then a member of the Government, produced an ambitious plan for conquering unemployment, which was rejected by Snowden because it did not conform with his own insistence on the maintenance of the Gold standard and a balanced budget. Mosley left the Government and continued to campaign for his plan outside, with the support of John Strachey, Aneurin Bevan and W. J. Brown. But when he was expelled from the party and formed his own New Party, Bevan, Brown and later Strachey, broke with him and Mosley went his own way, building up a blackshirt Mussolini-type fascist movement. The Government came under increasing pressure from the ILP and from the Communists, who were building up strength and influence, particularly among the intellectuals.

The crisis came to a head in the summer of 1931, with the publication of the May report, advocating drastic cuts in public expenditure, including a 20 per cent reduction in unemployment benefits. There was a run on sterling as foreign banks hastened to withdraw their holdings in Britain. Snowden refused to abandon his sacred cow, the Gold standard, and the Labour Cabinet and the TUC refused to accept the proposed cuts. MacDonald, already more at home with members of the Tory and Liberal benches than with his own side, failed to persuade the majority of the Cabinet to join him in a Coalition Government. In August 1931 MacDonald accepted the King's invitation to head a National government, taking with him Snowden, Lord Sankey and J. H. Thomas. The vast majority of his Cabinet refused to join him. At the fateful meeting on 24 August when MacDonald made his announcement – he had not consulted any of his colleagues – he was heard in stunned silence, broken by Herbert Morrison: 'Prime Minister, I think you are wrong . . . I for one am not coming with you.'

It was the end of MacDonald as a Labour leader, and it also seemed to be the end of the road for the party he deserted. The election that autumn, held in an atmosphere of Jingoist panic, resulted in a landslide 'National' victory. Labour's representation in Parliament dropped below fifty and ex-Ministers fell like ninepins. Only Lansbury, Cripps and Attlee survived. Almost half the party in the House consisted of miners' MPs and only South Wales remained completely loyal.

MacDonald, increasingly a prisoner of the Tories, lingered on, becoming more aloof and woolly and lost in Celtic mists, a meaningless figurehead of 'national unity'. He resigned in June 1935, handing over to Stanley Baldwin, was resoundingly beaten by Shinwell in the 1935 election and died in 1937.

The events leading up to the formation of the National Government have been fully chronicled in the memoirs of leading politicians and their biographers. The only excuse for recalling them here is because of the deep and lasting scars they left on the Labour Party. As Morrison wrote in his autobiography: 'The spiritual and psychological effects upon the Labour movement of what became known as "the great Betrayal" were as serious as the thing in itself and its immediate electoral consequences. It left in the party a spirit of distrust of the idea of leadership, a determination that for the time being there should be no more great men . . .' This thought was echoed by Citrine who wrote: 'Never again would a Labour Prime Minister be permitted to exercise such autocratic power.' What is surprising is that though his leadership was under attack at times from left, right and centre, nobody had the temerity to challenge MacDonald or even to stand against him for office. Perhaps there was secret agreement with Beatrice Webb's comment: 'He is the best man we've got to put in our shop window.'

MacDonald's leadership has provided his successors with a textbook example of how not to lead the Larbour Party. Apart from his personal characteristics of vanity, arrogance and ambition, he showed an utter contempt for the democratic processes of the party which contributed to turning the hero of the early 1920s into the villain of the 1930s. As Bevin later summed up: 'The great crime of Ramsay MacDonald was that he never called in his party.'

Arthur Henderson, much against his will, was 'drafted' into the Leadership in November 1931, although he had been defeated in the election. He was universally trusted and his honesty, modesty and loyalty were in striking contrast to MacDonald. But as he was spending much time in Geneva as President of the Disarmament conference and was in failing health, he resigned a year later and was succeeded by George Lansbury, the only surviving ex-Cabinet Minister. Lansbury, by then seventy-two, was a much-loved figure, but he was a sentimental, woolly-minded pacifist and intensely unhappy in the job. He admitted that he would rather be regarded as 'spokesman' than 'Leader' of the party. He was eventually driven from office by the blunt – some say unnecessarily cruel – tactics of Ernest Bevin at the Brighton party conference in 1935. Bevin accused him of 'hawking your conscience from body to body asking to be told what you ought to do with it'.

Lansbury could not have survived such an onslaught, and in any case it was obviously impossible for the party to be led by a pacifist at a time when collective security and defence against fascism were becoming burning issues. So he went, shortly before Baldwin called a general election.

The party was again faced with the agonising decision of having to choose a leader. There was a triangular contest between Attlee, who had been Lansbury's deputy, Herbert Morrison and Arthur Greenwood. On the first vote Attlee got 58 votes, Morrison 44 and Greenwood 33; on the second, Greenwood's votes were switched to Attlee who won 88 votes against Morrison's 44. Morrison was at a disadvantage in having been outside Parliament between 1931 and 1935, even though he had done stalwart work at the London County Council. He was mistrusted by Bevin and other trade union leaders.

Attlee was at the time described in the *New Statesman* as 'a natural adjutant, but not a general'. Churchill and the Tories were wont to dismiss him as a nonentity, but events proved how wrong they were. Attlee was the first non-working-class leader of the Labour Party – Haileybury- and Oxford-educated, he acquired his socialism by working in the East End of London. (Alf Robens once told me that the party would never again choose a man of working-class origins and elementary schooling as their leader.) Attlee led the party for twenty years.

He was broadly in charge of home affairs during the war-time Coalition, when Churchill was frequently away on his secret missions. Cabinet colleagues remember the speed with which Cabinet business was transacted and decisions reached under his chairmanship. As Prime Minister in his own right he could be tough and ruthless, particularly when it came to sacking a Minister who had not measured up to the job. His terse, unemotional manner, his wit and his guile made him a formidable opponent. His decision to grant Indian independence at a stroke – 'I decided the only thing to do was to set a time limit and say "whatever happens our rule is ending on that date",' he told Francis Williams – was an example of his capacity for incisive action. His own position, supported by the massive figure of Ernest Bevin, his Foreign Secretary, was unassailable. An attempt to unseat him in 1947, in which Cripps was deeply involved, was abortive. He was never a good mixer although he would unbend over a bottle of claret at dinner-time. Wilfred Fienburgh once said that conversation with Clem was like 'tossing biscuits to a dog and a very hungry dog at that'. A 'Yes' or 'No' were often the response to questions, and 'interesting' was his favourite adjective.

The 1945–50 Cabinet was a collection of political prima donnas – Bevin, Morrison, Cripps, Dalton and Aneurin Bevan – all extremely jealous of their position in the hierarchy and determined to safeguard the interests of their own department.

Attlee held this assorted crew together, and presented a united front to the Tories and the country. Bevin once told me: 'He has hardly ever made a constructive suggestion but by God he's the only man that could hold us together.'

The 1945–50 Government, now legend in Labour Party annals, managed to push through a staggering programme of economic and social reform, in accordance with its election pledges. Its measures included nationalisation of the mines, gas and electricity, the railways, the Bank of England and the air lines. A National Health Service was created and a new social security scheme introduced. The school-leaving age was raised and many new schools were built – the drive to build more houses was less successful. Up to 1947 the party did not lose a single by-election, but thereafter it encountered increasing difficulties on the economic and political fronts. R. H. S. Crossman has commented that the trouble was the Government 'ran out of steam'. Certainly after mid-1947 nothing seemed to go right. The Keep Left group in Parliament kept up a steady pressure on Bevin to change his foreign policy and end the Cold War. In the country generally there was growing resentment at continued austerity and rationing, and the Conservatives, under the guiding hand of Lord Woolton, were steadily improving their machinery.

There was also trouble on the labour front, particularly in the docks, where a series of protracted strikes, under Communist leadership, proved highly damaging to the economy. A foreign exchange crisis in the summer of 1947 obliged Cripps, who by then had become Supremo in the economic field, to bring in drastic restrictions on spending and wage restraint. Restraint was, broadly, accepted by the unions, both out of loyalty to the Government and because they accepted the overall fairness of its policies.

Attlee was not at his best at such times of internal party crisis. He did not give the firm leadership which the party and the country wanted, but tended to sit back and complete his doodles, or his *Times* crossword, while the arguments raged around him. He was also in very poor health. The 1950 election produced a swing against Labour, and its majority fell from 146 to 6. This margin was too small to allow the Government to introduce any far-reaching measures – in fact the election manifesto contained a hotch-potch of unrelated nationalisation proposals, including sugar, cement and water, and parts of the chemical industry. (Incidentally Harold Wilson, with an even smaller majority in 1964, promised an ambitious programme of social and industrial reform.)

The deaths of Cripps and Bevin robbed the Government of two of its most experienced senior Ministers and most members of the Cabinet were beginning to feel the strain of office. Attlee himself went into hospital at Easter 1951 and was unable to intervene in the conflict that flared up between Gaitskell (who had succeeded Cripps) and Bevan over the imposition of health charges. This conflict led to the resignation of Bevan, Harold Wilson and John Freeman and left the party leadership almost exclusively in right-wing hands. Morrison's period at the Foreign Office was a far from happy one. The Korean war placed new burdens on the economy and there was a general atmosphere of despair and disillusionment. Attlee called an election in the autumn of 1951 – much to the anger of Herbert Morrison, who was in the USA at the time the decision was made. The result was a Conservative victory, with a majority of seventeen, although Labour polled the highest number of votes on record.

As leader of the Opposition Attlee had to grapple with the most serious internal divisions that had ever wracked the party. The old Keep Left group was reformed, with Aneurin Bevan as its titular head and a state amounting to civil war developed between the group and the right-wing leadership. A revolt of fifty-seven Labour MPs over rearmament in March 1952 resulted in the re-imposition of party discipline, so that any rebel MP risked suspension, if not expulsion.

Attlee disliked public slanging matches and visibly quailed when at the Morecambe conference that year Will Lawther shouted to a heckler 'Shut your gob' and Deakin made a rude, Harvey Smith, gesture to Bevan. Deakin later publicly rebuked Attlee for not being firm enough in his handling of the Bevanite 'disruptionists'. Attlee was unhappy and unwilling to wield the big stick. When Bevan had transgressed to such an extent that the question of withdrawing the Whip came before the Shadow Cabinet in 1955, Attlee said 'I'm against expulsion', took no part in the discussion and concluded with the words 'I'm against drastic action'. The decision to withdraw the Whip was reached by 141 votes to 112. At the National Executive Committee meeting held to consider Bevan's expulsion, Attlee put forward a compromise scheme, saving Bevan from the hatchet-men of the right by allowing him to remain in the party if he made an apology. It was carried by one vote.

Why, everybody asked, did Attlee not act sooner, or make his compromise suggestion at the Shadow Cabinet meeting? It was surely a negation of leadership to allow things to go so far, when earlier action might have prevented the crisis. It was, however, his practice to lie low and say nuffin, like Brer Rabbit. As Morrison put it, 'he doodled when he ought to have led'.

From then on there was a revival of the AMG (Attlee Must Go) movement, although the Bevanites were determined to see their protector remain at the helm. Attlee, by now sixty-eight, was growing increasingly disinterested in party politics. The 1955 election produced the second defeat running for the party, which dropped over 1½ million in votes, while the Tories increased their majority from seventeen to fifty-eight. The Campaign had been dispirited and dispiriting, and it was significant that there was no contact during it between Attlee, Morrison, Griffiths and the party chairman Edith Summerskill. The election manifesto, 'Forward with Labour' was uninspiring and had been dubbed by Nye Bevan as 'cold porridge pushed through a blanket'.

Yet, even after the defeat, Attlee showed no signs of going. There is plenty of evidence that his main motive in remaining was to make sure that Morrison did not get the succession. He bowed out suddenly in December 1955, at a time when it was clear that Gaitskell's star was rising and Morrison's waning. He himself said there was need for younger men at the top. 'We must have men brought up in the present age and not, as I was, in the Victorian age' he told Percy Cudlipp in a *News Chronicle* interview. He once told me that to him 'The War' was not Hitler's war, nor even the Kaiser's, but the Boer War.

As party leader, Attlee regarded himself as 'left of centre – which is where a party leader ought to be'. The man who succeeded him, Hugh Gaitskell, was definitely right of centre.

F

True, when he was elected, he said he agreed with Attlee that the leader should be 'a little left of centre', but this assurance did not satisfy the Bevanites, who still regarded him as an apostle of the right and the principal villain in the plot to expel Bevan.

Gaitskell was forty-nine when he succeeded Attlee. He won a decisive victory, the first time round, with 157 votes to Bevan's seventy and Morrison's forty. It was the end of Morrison as an active politician – he never recovered from the blow to his pride. Gaitskell had the backing of the big union leaders, who had never forgiven Morrison from 'running away' from the Treasurership, and in Parliament he had a large following among both moderate and right-wing MPs. His impassioned declaration of his socialist faith at the party conference that year had marked him out as a future leader and Nye Bevan's dismissal of it as 'sheer demagoguery' was not the view of the vast majority of delegates.

Bevan, who had transferred his hostility from Morrison to Gaitskell, was in no mood to be co-operative. He wanted to become Party Treasurer and he wanted to become Shadow Foreign Minister. Both these jobs fell into his lap the following year, and a rapprochement between the two men began to develop. The Suez affair cemented the alliance, with Gaitskell, if anything, even more passionate in his denunciation of the Tory adventure. The reconciliation was completed at Brighton in 1957, when Bevan parted company with his erstwhile supporters. He spoke for the National Executive against a resolution calling for the unilateral renunciation by Britain of the H-bomb, using the famous and much-quoted phrase, 'If you carry this resolution, you will send a Foreign Secretary, whoever he may be, naked into the conference chamber.'

Despite improvements in party organisation and the newly found unity at the top, Labour lost the 1959 election after a vigorous campaign in which the electorate were impressed by Gaitskell's sincerity, but unwilling to risk their newly found affluence by voting Labour. 'The future Labour offers you' proved less attractive than Macmillan's status quo slogan 'You've never had it so good' and the Conservatives were returned with an increased majority. The Labour Party seemed weaker and more dispirited than at any time since 1931 and there were fears that the old internecine feuds would break out all over again. Indeed they did, over Clause Four and Unilateralism. Gaitskell's action on both these issues is described elsewhere.

The party after 1961 showed a surprising ability to close its ranks and there was a revival of morale, which coincided with a slump in Conservative fortunes.

The tragic death of Aneurin Bevan in 1960 was followed less than three years later by that of Gaitskell. Gaitskell died at the height of his ascendancy and there seemed every prospect that he would lead his party to election victory.

When a man dies people ask a host of unanswerable and therefore pointless questions about what might have been. So with Hugh Gaitskell – would he have won the 1964 election and with a bigger majority than Wilson's? Would he have made a good Prime Minister? What would he have done about prices and incomes? Would he have changed his mind about British entry into Europe? And so on.

Gaitskell would certainly have won the 1964 election, probably by about the same margin as Wilson. Able and dedicated as he was I do not think he could have held the party together in the same way that Harold Wilson has done. To substantiate this judgement one must look at his background and character.

Hugh Naylor Todd Gaitskell was born in 1906, the son of an Indian civil servant and was educated at Winchester and New College, Oxford, where he read philosophy, politics and economics. He first became a socialist in the 1920s, when he saw the effects of poverty and deprivation on the workers and their families. His first practical act was to drive a car for the local strike committee during the General Strike, when most of his contemporaries were driving trains and lorries for the other side. After a period of lecturing in economics at London, in which he mingled with the Bloomsbury set, he joined Hugh Dalton at the Ministry of Economic Warfare, on the outbreak of war. He stood for Parliament in 1935 but did not get elected until 1945, when he almost immediately became Parliamentary Secretary at the Ministry of Fuel – and after the fuel crisis of 1947, its Minister. A protegé of Cripps, he was made Minister of State at the Treasury and Chancellor of the Exchequer when Sir Stafford retired through ill-health. He at once clashed with Bevan, who was furious at being passed over for high office by a man so much his junior and not a real 'socialist' at that.

An economist and intellectual, Gaitskell was often accused of arrogance and coldness. This was the origin of Bevan's jibe about a 'desiccated calculating machine' (which he later denied as being a reference to Gaitskell). This was a misjudgement. Gaitskell was a rather shy person, but warm-hearted, compassionate and capable of deep emotion. He wept at a miners' conference at Porthcawl, when the country was threatened with a financial crisis – I can vouch for this, for I was at the press table. He was extremely sensitive to criticism from the press, which he disliked and never tried to cultivate. He took great pleasure in the arts, and the get-togethers on Sunday mornings at his Hampstead home (the target of much left-wing criticism) were frequented by artists and writers, as well as by politicians and economists. He loved dancing and was equally at ease in a Viennese waltz and a rock and roll session.

Nobody questioned his sincerity and integrity, but doubts were often raised about his political judgement and sense of timing (for example in raising the Clause Four controversy before the scars of election defeat had even begun to heal). He was stubborn and inflexible, over-meticulous and unwilling to delegate, and not an infallible judge of people. Yet, as his great friend Roy Jenkins wrote, ten years after his death (*The Times*, 20 January 1973): 'When these faults are put in the scales and weighed against his qualities they shrivel away. He had purpose and direction, courage and humanity . . . His own leadership . . . was infused by sense and humour and by a desire to change the world, not for his own satisfaction, but so that people might more enjoy living in it.'

Harold Wilson, who had been working increasingly closely with Gaitskell since 1961 and had been made his Shadow Chancellor, succeeded as leader in 1963. He secured a decisive victory over his two opponents, George Brown and James Callaghan. The voting in the first ballot was Wilson

115, Brown 88, Callaghan 41, and in the second ballot Wilson secured 144 votes against Brown's 103. He was the obvious choice for leader. He had long Parliamentary experience and was a brilliant House of Commons performer; he had been the youngest Minister ever in the Attlee Government, first at Works and later at the Board of Trade. He was acceptable to the left, who recalled his Bevanite links, and to the moderates who hoped that he would succeed in burying the old feuds and re-uniting the party against the Conservatives. The Tories were on the defensive. The Profumo scandal and the squabbles over the succession to Macmillan combined to give the nation an impression of an administration which, after nearly thirteen years, was tired and torpid. Wilson brought a breath of fresh air into the foetid political atmosphere. He was ready to offer the electorate something new and exciting in his plans to harness the resources of science and technology for the benefit of the nation. In his speech at the Scarborough conference 1963 he declared: 'We are re-defining and we are re-stating our Socialism in terms of the scientific revolution . . . The Britain that is going to be forged in the white heat of this revolution will be no place for restrictive practices or for outdated methods on either side of industry.'

Wilson's 'new vision' was loudly applauded by the delegates, including many trade unionists who would never be able or willing to change their traditional and defensive attitudes. After the long years in the wilderness and the interminable internal wrangling, he offered a break with the past and the party enthusiastically accepted his leadership.

The 1964 election was fought almost entirely on economic and social affairs, with the end of 'Stop-go' policies as the main theme. Wilson had a clear lead in the public opinion polls and Transport House propaganda made good use of his popularity. The party was put at some disadvantage by the Conservatives' decision to postpone the election date till almost the last possible minute – Wilson had expected a spring election and his plans had been geared to this. However, when it did come, in the autumn, Labour was returned, not by the comfortable majority it had hoped for, but by the tiny overall margin of four seats.

The narrowness of his Parliamentary majority did not deter the new Prime Minister from proceeding as if he had received an overwhelming mandate to govern. He rejected outright all ideas of coalition with the Liberals and announced that the first 100 days would set the pattern. 'The Government have only a small majority in the House of Commons', he said in a nation-wide TV broadcast. 'I want to make it quite clear that this will not affect our ability to govern. Having been charged with the duties of Government we intend to carry out those duties.'

The record of the two Wilson administrations 1964–70 were examined in Chapter III. Here it is only necessary to take a look at Wilson's style of leadership in Government and in opposition. He accepted the Attlee doctrine of leading from the left of centre, a position which he himself had always occupied in the party, but was shrewd enough to realise the need not to alienate the right. His main concern throughout has been to maintain the coalition and preserve party unity. In his first Cabinet he dished out appointments with equal generosity to left, right and centre. George Brown, James Callaghan, Denis Healey, Ray Gunter, Frank Cousins, Barbara Castle, Dick Crossman and Tony Greenwood – a Ministry of all the talents and of all shades of political opinions.

Wilson, like Gaitskell, had come to the House of Commons via the Civil service, having been a chief statistician in the wartime Ministry of Fuel and Power. Born in 1916, he was educated at council and grammar school, and went to Jesus College, Oxford, later becoming a Fellow of All Souls.

He rose rapidly in the party, becoming a junior Minister at twenty-nine, President of the Board of Trade at thirty-one and was the youngest Prime Minister, at forty-eight, since William Pitt. Despite his academic success and intellectual brilliance, Harold Wilson never lost his feel for the working-class. His pipe, his mackintosh and his HP sauce, a gift to the cartoonists, presented a comfortable re-assurance to his supporters that he, at any rate, would never 'do a MacDonald' on them and succumb to the blandishments of London society. A brilliant Parliamentarian, with a mordant wit and an uncanny memory for facts and figures, he is a formidable adversary in debate, as Ted Heath has found many times to his cost. Although he frequently attacks the 'media', Wilson is fully aware of the importance of the press and TV and, at any rate in the early days of his Government, was on extremely good terms with the Lobby journalists. He is an assiduous student of the papers and the opinion polls.

It is always difficult to assess a man's contribution to public life when he is still in the full stream of his career. Wilson has had many critics, and there has been at least one move to oust him from the leadership. His tendency to compromise, in the interests of party unity, has been interpreted as a sign of inconsistency and deviousness. His habit of playing his cards close to his chest and his 'personal' style of leadership caused the departure from the Government of Ray Gunter and George Brown. He was, however, far less ruthless than Attlee when it came to dismissing members of his Cabinet and it was often said that he allowed obvious misfits to remain because he did not like sacking them. He tended to govern on a day-to-day basis – this was perhaps inevitable when each day produced a new crisis – but he could be stubborn, as for example his refusal to devalue the pound until November 1967.

After the 1959 defeat Gaitskell plunged into policy-making right away, whereas after June 1970 Wilson bided his time, writing his memoirs instead of seeking to rally the faithful and restore party morale. It was only in late 1972 that the 'old' Wilson began to re-emerge. His tightrope walking over Europe at the Blackpool conference, his thoughtful policy speech at Edinburgh and his devastating onslaught on Heath's prices and incomes policy, Stage 2, put paid to any lingering ideas that he might not lead the party into the next election.

In any case the absence of an obvious and acceptable alternative made him, in the eyes of most Labour supporters, 'the best next Prime Minister we've got'. It is another fruitless but enjoyable political game to pick out future party leaders or to speculate on what would happen if the present leader were to fall under the proverbial bus.

There is nobody on the Labour front bench who

immediately springs to mind. James Callaghan might be the obvious choice, but he is not popular with the left, and is too much in Wilson's own age group. The same applies to Denis Healey, although his stock has risen among MPs. Roy Jenkins probably ruled himself out of court by his resignation and by becoming identified with European policies. Barbara Castle never lived down 'In place of strife' and it is unlikely that Labour MPs would ever pick a woman leader – which would also rule out Shirley Williams. Anthony Wedgwood Benn is regarded as too volatile.

Possible runners, whose names have been mentioned, are Reg Prentice, the spokesman on labour affairs, but he alienated left-wing trade unionists by his appeal to the locomen to go back to normal working in March 1973. This probably leaves deputy leader Edward Short as the front-runner. He is little known to the public but has a good record within the party for commonsense and tolerance.

VIII

Leaders and led

The question of the relationship between the party conference and the Parliamentary Labour Party was posed sharply after the 1970 General Election. Put in the simplest terms it is: How far should MPs be bound by conference decisions? One school of thought, currently represented by Tony Wedgwood Benn, who believes in the 'infallibility' of conference to arrive at correct decisions, is that its will must prevail. The other view, expressed by Douglas Houghton, is that MPs are elected to represent their constituents as a whole and cannot be made accountable to party conference.

Houghton and his friends are fond of quoting Edmund Burke's dictum that all an MP owes to his constituents is the value of his judgement. 'Your representative owes you not his industry only, but his judgement and he betrays instead of serving you if he sacrifices it to your opinion.' The Tribune group dismissed Burke as 'old hat'. 'We do not live in Burke's world any more and it is time the PLP understood that the aristocratic concepts which ruled these islands in the eighteenth century are unfitted for a modern democracy.'

The problem is as old as the Labour Party itself. As long ago as 1907, the year after the Labour Representation Committee was transformed into the Labour Party, seventeen resolutions were put forward at annual conference, seeking to bind Parliamentarians to accept conference 'instructions'. Most people in the party regard Keir Hardie as the fount of all wisdom and accept his dicta as gospel. Yet, at this conference, he actually threatened to resign over a motion on women's suffrage, saying that 'if the motion was intended to limit the action of the party in the House of Commons, he would have seriously to consider whether he remained a member of the Parliamentary party'. (In early days conferences were reported in indirect speech.) Hardie's own view was: 'In the House of Commons the membership of the party decide their own policy without interference from the Executive or any outside authority.' No doubt the Tribune group would have regarded this statement, if made today, as heresy.

The Executive Committee, on the initiative of Arthur Henderson, proposed a formula that: 'Resolutions instructing the Parliamentary party as to their action in the House of Commons be taken as the opinions of the conference, on the understanding that the time and method of giving effect to these instructions be left to the party in the House, in conjunction with the National Executive.'

This rather less than explicit statement has broadly remained operative ever since that day, but there has been continuous controversy over its interpretation.

In 1920, Emmanuel (now Lord) Shinwell described the PLP as 'the property of the Labour movement' and called for it to be subject to party decisions. J. R. Clynes, the chairman, reaffirmed the independence of the PLP and said that Shinwell 'did not know as much as he thought he knew about the things he criticised'.

Ramsay MacDonald in 1928 declared that 'as long as he held any position in the Parliamentary party, they were not going to take their instructions from any outside body unless they agreed with them'. One can imagine the outcry that would arise in modern times if the Party Leader described conference as an 'outside body', but there is no evidence that any protests were voiced at MacDonald's statement. Philip Snowden went even further: 'Conferences will talk; let them talk. Governments dispose of conference resolutions. There is all the difference in the world between the licence and irresponsibility of a conference and the position of a Government which has to face practical difficulties . . .'

Clem Attlee, who became leader in 1935, was a bit ambivalent on this issue. In the debate on Defence estimates in 1936, he said: 'The Parliamentary party has full control over the carrying out of decisions of party conference and party policy in the House of Commons.' In his book *The Labour Party in Perspective* he wrote that conference 'lays down the policy of the party and issues instructions which must be carried out by the Executive, the affiliated organisations and its representatives in Parliament and on local authorities'.

He was to take a rather different view of the position when Labour was in office. This was shown in his correspondence with Churchill over the Laski incident in 1945. Churchill had invited Attlee and Bevin to attend the Potsdam conference, due to be held after polling day but before the announcement of results. Harold Laski, then NEC chairman, issued a statement that Attlee should attend 'in the rôle of an observer only'. Attlee accepted Churchill's invitation and repudiated Laski's intervention. Churchill wrote to Attlee: 'It certainly appears that they (the powers vested in the Executive) are very wide in their terms and very real. It would appear that a Labour or Socialist Government would be subject to the directions of this Committee and that matters of foreign affairs and also I presume if they desired it, military affairs, would have to be submitted to them. So far as I am now informed they have a right to be consulted and to express opinions which are binding on the Ministers or a Socialist Government or on the Cabinet itself. I feel that the situation is extremely disquieting.'

Quintin Hogg was even more virulent about the NEC and warned: '. . . never since the days of Cromwell has a single force in this country constituted a more formidable menace to political liberty'.

To Churchill Attlee replied in his typically terse manner. 'The new position with which you state we are confronted exists only in your imagination. Neither by decision of the annual party conference nor by any provision in the party constitution is the Parliamentary Labour Party answerable to, or under the direction of the National Executive . . . At no time and in no circumstances has the NEC ever sought to give or given instructions to the Parliamentary Labour Party arising out of consultations. Indeed it has no power to do so.' The sting was in the tail: 'I am sorry that you should have been so distressed owing to your lack of acquaintance with the procedure of democratic parties in general and of the Labour Party in particular.'

The Laski incident has been recalled at some length because it foreshadowed what was to become the subsequent pattern of the Attlee Government. During the 1945–50 period, the National Executive Committee took a back seat and rarely asserted its independent existence. As for the rôle of conference, Aneurin Bevan, when Minister of Housing, two years running rejected a conference demand designed to commit the Government to abolish the tied cottage.

'It is quite impossible for a conference of 1,100 people, even if it were constitutionally proper, to determine the order in which the Parliamentary Labour Party and the Government introduces legislation into the House of Commons. . . . All the conference can do is to record its views on principle and ask that they be implemented at the earliest possible moment.' On both occasions, 1947 and 1948, the conference carried the resolutions against the advice of Nye Bevan.

There were mutterings from the left that the conference and the NEC had abdicated their 'historic rôle' and had merely become rubber-stamps to Government decisions. But these complaints were never pressed very far and in any case the leadership could always rely on the support of the big unions, under their right-wing leaders, to suppress any embarrassing rebellious tendencies.

Relationships between leaders and led are rather different when the party is in Opposition. In the early 1950s ex-Ministers felt themselves bound to defend policies with which they had been associated, but such hang-over inhibitions are usually short-lived and were markedly absent after 1970. In periods of Opposition, more attention is paid to conference resolutions and to the rôle of the NEC in campaigning against Government measures. There is no longer the same moral obligation to back the leadership at all costs.

But, especially if an election is approaching, the sense of future responsibility weighs heavily on the leaders. Hugh Gaitskell successfully challenged the right of party conference to lay down foreign policy. At Scarborough, in 1960, the nuclear disarmers triumphed with a hair's breadth majority of 43,000. Gaitskell threw down the gauntlet. In his much-quoted speech to conference he defended the right of MPs to make their own decisions: 'It is not in dispute that the vast majority of Labour Members of Parliament are utterly opposed to unilateralism and neutralism. So what do you expect them to do? To go back on the pledges they gave to the people who elected them from their constituencies? ... I do not believe that Labour Members of Parliament are prepared to act as time-servers ... because they are men of conscience and honour ... There are some of us who will fight and fight and fight again to save the party we love. We will fight and fight and fight again and bring back sanity and honesty and dignity, so that our party with its past may retain its glory and its greatness.'

Within a year the tables were turned. An effective campaign for Democratic Socialism, which owed much to its adoption of Tribune tactics, succeeded in reversing the Scarborough decision at Blackpool in 1961.

This not only established Gaitskell's ascendancy, but it reasserted the Parliamentary Party's independence of action.

About this time Morgan Phillips, the party secretary, in a special report re-stated the constitutional position, much on the lines of the 1907 statement: 'The Parliamentary party cannot for long remain at loggerheads with the annual conference without disrupting the party ... On the other hand the Parliamentary party cannot maintain its position in the country if it could be demonstrated that it was at any time or in any way subject to dictation from an outside body which, however representative of the party, could not be regarded as representative of the country.' The answer, he stressed, lay in 'mutual trust and confidence' between the various bodies.

Harold Wilson, though not a unilateralist, stood against Gaitskell for the leadership in 1960, largely in protest over Gaitskell's defiance of conference. He called on the party 'to repudiate the campaign now being waged ... for a major change in the democratic and socialist basis of the movement'. 'If Hugh Gaitskell were returned unopposed', he said, 'this will be taken as a mandate from his parliamentary colleagues to defy conference, to ignore the National Executive Committee and to plunge the movement into still worse conflict.'

When Wilson himself became leader he managed, by a

combination of deftness and diplomacy, to heal the breach. With the Tories on the run and an election in the offing the party had neither the time nor the inclination to pursue doctrinal controversies about the internal balance of power. In 1964–6 the Labour Government had a knife-edge majority and all efforts were concentrated on maintaining it in Parliament. After the 1966 victory which allowed a comfortable margin for dissent the old tensions began to develop and the familiar protests that the Government was by-passing conference and the NEC were again raised.

Wilson went even further than Attlee in refusing to submit to conference decisions. He accepted that conferences influenced policy, but, as he wrote in *The Relevance of British Socialism* (1964), 'It is not the function either of the conference or of the NEC to dictate to the Parliamentary Labour Party, still less to a Labour Government . . . the PLP is not bound automatically to accept any particular conference decision. And when a Labour Government is in power, it is well understood that no conference decision can be binding upon it'.

After the defeat of June 1970, delegates to party conference complained bitterly about the way in which conference and the NEC had been by-passed by the Government.

The mover of a composite resolution to this effect listed the re-introduction of prescription charges, the deflationary policies, the failure to dissociate Britain from the Vietnam war and the intervention in trade union affairs as examples. 'These were all issues against our election manifesto and conference decisions . . . If our leaders regard themselves as a privileged elite indulging in platform platitudes, flaunting our decisions, they will lead us to destruction,' he said. Another speaker complained: 'I think that what we all resent most is . . . that we have been treated with a cynicism in the rejection of conference decisions.'

The debate rumbled on, but it was not until late 1971 that it emerged as a really critical and divisive issue. The conflict came to a head on 28 October when sixty-nine Labour MPs voted with the Conservatives in favour of entry into the Common Market, defying the party Whip and ignoring conference decisions.

In the summer of 1972, the Tribune group of MPs published a pamphlet 'Labour: party or puppet?' which discussed questions of MPs' accountability and their relations with conference and the NEC. Among its specific proposals it suggested that the leader should be elected by annual conference and the position of deputy leader abolished.

One of its major concerns was to see that MPs toed the conference line. 'There is no reason whatever for allowing the Parliamentary party to continue exercising its present degree of independence ... The leadership and the Parliamentary party do not own the party and in the final analysis they must be accountable to the party.' To this end it recommended that newly elected candidates should sign an undertaking to carry out the party programme and policy as decided by conference and abide by Standing Orders, as approved by conference. The NEC would provide the PLP with an up-to-date guide to conference decisions at each Parliamentary session and all votes within the PLP which sought to overturn conference decisions would be conducted by a roll-call vote, which would be made available to local Labour parties, as well as to the NEC.

Not surprisingly MPs of the right and centre reacted strongly against the Tribune proposals. Douglas Houghton wrote in *The Political Quarterly* (October-December 1972): 'If all that comes about the PLP will be bound hand and foot ... The simple and overwhelming case against the Tribune Group and the conference resolutions is surely that they would make Labour unfit to govern.'

Houghton was referring to a series of resolutions for the party conference calling on Labour MPs to abide by conference decisions – or get out. A composite resolution on these lines was not, however, debated at Blackpool and it was left to Ian Mikardo and the Tribune group to carry on the campaign in the columns of Tribune and elsewhere. Speaking in London on 10 November, Mikardo warned that Labour was split in a new dimension: 'It almost looks as though some Labour MPs and especially those with an elitist, condescending attitude towards the rank and file of the party, are taking a perverse pleasure in throwing down a gauntlet of defiance of the party members and the annual conference.'

Ron Hayward, exercising his right as general secretary to speak at Parliamentary party meetings, told MPs: 'It would be a very foolish Parliamentary Labour Party that did not take serious note of what the NEC and the annual conference decided.'

In the increasingly bitter atmosphere which developed during 1972 it became difficult to detect the elements of 'mutual trust and confidence' which Morgan Phillips had described as the cornerstone of the relationships between the PLP, and NEC and the conference.

IX

Participation

Labour's vote-winning election manifesto of 1945 was drafted almost single-handed by Herbert Morrison, then chairman of the party's home policy committee. Morrison consulted a few colleagues and sympathetic journalists, mainly from the *Daily Mirror*, but, as he made clear in his autobiography[1] it was essentially a one-man effort. 'My primary and personal duty in this (policy) committee was to draft for its consideration a policy declaration for the coming election. This I did and gave it the title "Let us face the future".'

Twenty-five years and seven general elections later, the party adopted a very different technique. The strategy projected by the National Executive for the new policy statement was to involve as many people as possible on the broadest possible basis. 'Participation' became the inword of the 1970s. There had been repeated complaints that the leaders had lost touch with the rank and file, which had caused many supporters to vote with their bedroom slippers and stay at home.

The party, during the years of the Wilson Government, had been happily free from the bitter personal controversies of the 1950s which had contributed so much to successive election defeats, but there was mounting criticism, and not only from the left, that the Government was high-handed and had failed to consult the elected National Executive, or to pay any attention to conference decisions. A 'We' and 'They' attitude developed, as the feeling grew that the

[1] *Herbert Morrison, An Autobiography* (Odhams 1960). Morrison does not record that Ian Mikardo in 1944 moved a successful resolution calling for explicit commitment to public ownership to be included in the Manifesto, in order 'to put some teeth in it, to put some Socialism in it' as he (Mikardo) told the party conference in 1970.

Government was kicking away the ladder on which it had climbed to power.

The election defeat of June 1970 gave fresh impetus to a move that had already been mooted in 1969 – namely to improve the relations between the leaders and the local parties by involving the rank and file in policy discussion. The campaign was launched under the somewhat off-putting title 'Participation 1970'. In January 1970, according to an official party report, about 3,000 people in 250 groups discussed the question of 'Women and social security'. A second project, involving the discussion of economic equality, was planned but postponed because of the election. All this was reported to the 1970 conference at Blackpool, where 'participation' was the subject of debate. Though brief and inconclusive – it was only reached in the Friday morning rush – the discussion nevertheless showed the extent of resentment among constituency workers at having been neglected for so long.

There were two parallel, but dissimilar, resolutions. One called on the NEC to 'examine and recommend ways in which the Labour Party, trade unions, Co-operative Party and other socialist organisations might involve themselves in community action proposals'. The other wanted 'greater participation by the general public in the decisions which affect them'. Both resolutions were adopted and 'participation' thus became official party policy.

Typical of the attitude of local party members was the speech of Mr George Taylor, Islington East. He agreed that too many constituency parties were 'inward-looking and claustrophobic' but said: 'It appears to me that the NEC are all in favour of participation in decision-making everywhere except in the internal affairs of this party (applause) ... At present the upper reaches of this party seem to resemble a vast bed where the privileged indulge in an orgy of self-congratulation, while participation is by invitation only. The rest of us want to join in the fun.'

'Unless we are given greater participation in the decision-making of this party's policy, then we have become meaningless as a party – we no longer exist', was another view. A trade union delegate, however, said it was 'all bunkum' to say that people did not have the chance to participate – all they had to do was to take a more active part in their union and party branches. Replying for the Executive, Tom Bradley, President of the Transport Salaried Staffs Association, gave a pledge that the necessary action would be taken. 'Real and genuine participation must be secured in every aspect of our industrial and community life, for without it we can never achieve power . . . The promotion of a functioning and healthy democracy is one of the great challenges of the decade.'

The debate provided, at the least, a healthy opportunity for delegates to let off steam. At the most it was a salutary reminder to the leadership that they must keep in touch with opinion in local parties, and give the activists, who after all keep the party going between elections and bear the main brunt of campaigning, a sense of partnership.

Now enter Anthony Wedgwood Benn, MP for Bristol Southeast and chairman of the party in 1971–2. It fell to him to try and translate these somewhat platitudinous aspirations into concrete terms and to produce a broader definition or participation than the limited exercise of 1969. 'Participation 1972' was the result. Benn himself prefers to call it 'democracy'.

Tony Wedgwood Benn has often been dubbed Labour's 'whizzkid' by the popular papers, because even in his late forties he preserved his youthful appearance and effervescence. The eldest son of Lord Stansgate, a former Labour Minister, Benn first made his reputation by his long and tenacious Parliamentary fight to remain a Commoner. His success introduced a new element into British politics and provided an escape hatch for eldest sons who do not want to become peers. He succeeded to Sir Stafford Cripps' seat in 1950 and was appointed Postmaster-General and later Minister of Technology, by Harold Wilson. In both Ministries he showed a grasp of the complexities of modern technology and an ability to translate them into language people can understand. His theme throughout has been: 'People want technology, but it must be technology with a human face.'

Under Benn's chairmanship, the initiative to inject more

democracy into party affairs and extend consultation took several forms.

First the NEC invited secretaries of all local parties, trade unions and socialist societies to hold special meetings to discuss priorities and policies for the next programme. These views, the groups were assured, would be taken into account in drafting a programme for presentation to the 1972 conference, which would eventually form the basis of an election manifesto.

Secondly, Benn said he wanted to 'see to it that as many people as possible are able to join in this policy thinking, not only within the party, but even more broadly'. Disillusionment with the two main political parties did not at first benefit the Liberals, but took the form of people turning to sources of pressure other than Parliament. The success of the Cublington lobby against the third airport plan and the revolt of the residents of Acland Road over Westway motorway were two examples of successful pressure groups. In the late 1960s and early 1970s the trend, especially among young people, was to take part in protest demonstrations, marches, sit-ins, but not under the aegis of any particular party.

Benn's idea was to see some of this ferment of activity and protest channelled into constructive social purposes and to let the Labour Party offer a capacious umbrella for the airing of opinions. He sought to enlist the services of various outside groups in advising on those aspects of policy with which they were particularly associated. Many such groups already arrange tea-parties or evening meetings at party conferences – it is all rather like the Edinburgh Festival where the 'fringe' activities often attract as much attention as the formal proceedings. He did not draw the line at groups which have natural links with the party, such as the Fabian Society, Tribune, Socialist Commentary and the associations of labour lawyers, doctors and farmers. He wanted to include such social pressure groups as Shelter, Oxfam, Child Poverty Action and organisations representing the interests of women, old-age pensioners, immigrants, consumers, the disabled and mentally handicapped, as well as the Churches and synagogues. 'Why not add Women's Lib and the "gay" groups?' commented one sceptical party official.

This was the first time that any political party had spread its net so wide in its search for ideas and opinions. Benn added a cautious note. Nobody would be committed to anything and it would just be a 'consultative relationship in which we can keep each other informed'. His Grand Design had much in common with Robert Owen's grandiose (but abortive) conceptions of concerted action to promote industrial democracy in the 1830s. It remains to be seen whether his strategy will eventually prove more successful.

The third element in the situation was the determination to restore harmony and co-operation between the industrial and political wings of the movement. We have already looked at the structural relationships and at the growing gap between them after 1966 (see Chapters II and V). Benn told the Fabian Society in the autumn of 1971: 'The party when in power alienated the most important pressure group of all from it – the British trade union movement. We now need their energy and they now need our leadership if we are to succeed.'

It is easy to dismiss Wedgwood Benn's ideas as 'gimmickry' and to make fun of his idealism. His enthusiasm made a refreshing change from the general mood of cynicism and apathy that prevailed in the opening years of the decade.

A writer in *Socialist Commentary*, the middle-of-the-road Jenkinsite journal, said in January 1972: 'We all owe a debt of gratitude to the chairman of the Labour Party for bringing the issue of democracy into the forefront of political debate.' But he was worried about Benn's conception of political leadership and his insistence on the binding character of conference decisions.

Benn's own chairmanship at Blackpool that year, when he vacillated between tolerance and authoritarianism, and his final outburst against the mass media, did not enhance his reputation within the party.

The most outspoken misgivings about the policy-making exercise were expressed by David Wood, political editor of *The Times* (3 January 1972): 'The democratic claims made for the policy-making exercise are moonshine . . . "Participation 72" is not only an extraordinary confession of political bankruptcy. It is also a drumhead court-martial of Mr Wilson and other principal members of the Cabinet he led, and consequently as it will turn out, another seedy manoeuvre in the struggle to change the Labour leadership or to put the Labour leadership in a straitjacket ... So the leadership must be passed to the led ... It would be profoundly worrying, but for the knowledge that when Labour comes back to power, "Participation 72" will be seen for the bogus and highly disposable public relations exercise it is.' The exercise nevertheless went ahead, as planned.

Throughout the spring of 1972 local Labour groups held special meetings to discuss the points raised in the 'Participation '72' questionnaire which had been circulated throughout the movement. In all 600 replies were received from constituency parties, local parties, wards, trades councils and other organisations. Transport House estimated that at least 800 meetings were held and some 10,000 party members directly involved in the exercise. I was able to sit in at some of these meetings, ranging from wards in big cities to rural constituency parties. In some places there was a good attendance and considerable interest and enthusiasm was engendered – people liked the chance to 'join in the fun'. Elsewhere there was only a handful of members who regarded the whole business as a rather time-wasting exercise when they ought to have been out canvassing, arranging jumble sales or preparing for the local elections. Everywhere I heard complaints about the shortage of time allowed – only about five weeks – to arrange meetings to discuss the project.

Members were presented with a long list of subjects, twenty-four in all, and asked to rate them according to their priority as 'Very important', 'Important', 'Not so important'.

The covering letter sent out by Sir Harry Nicholas, then the party's general secretary, explained that the purpose of 'Participation '72' was 'to give all party members the chance to comment on the issues we should study (in order that) our new party programme be comprehensive, relevant and forward-looking.' The leadership wanted the rank and file views on 'priority areas of policy that need to be included in this first draft programme'.

This emphasis on priorities is fundamental to Labour Party thinking. It was Nye Bevan who first proclaimed that 'the language of priorities is the religion of socialism' – a phrase to be quoted over and over again. Echoing Bevan's words, Jim Callaghan, speaking for the National Executive at the Blackpool conference in 1972 said: 'Socialism is not just a rag bag of needs, it is about priorities, and if this movement is to win not only the next election, which may be relatively easy, but the election after, when we have to match the promises that we make by deeds, then what we need from you is an indication of what your view is about priorities.'

'Participation '72' was not discussed at the conference, and there was little reference to it in the NEC report. But the results were reported to the Executive in June and showed the following order of priorities:

A summary of the six top priorities gives manpower and unemployment a clear lead over all other subjects, followed by education, housing, prices, taxation and social security (in that order). The absence of interest in foreign affairs, the burning topic of the early 1960s, is remarkable. On this the NEC report comments: 'If we are to regard this apathy as undesirable – and since socialism is an international movement we can have little choice – then it is clear that the NEC will have to embark on an extensive programme of information for Party members in this respect.' Surprisingly enough, the mass media, so often the target of virulent abuse at party conferences, received very low rating, as did consumer protection and the environment.

Admittedly there was nothing very scientific or methodical about the way in which the 'poll' was conducted. In some places the priorities were decided on a show of hands and in others it was left to the secretary or chairman to draw up a report on the consensus of opinion. Many subjects were omitted from the list which might have been regarded as of considerable importance, for example the Common Market, Northern Ireland, transport, health, incomes (as distinct from prices) policy, immigration, the land and population.

This was the result reported to the NEC in June 1972:

Priority position of all issues—Per cent

	1st	2nd	3rd	4th	5th	6th
Agriculture	—	—	—	—	5·1	5·7
Public expenditure	10·5	5·7	7·0	4·0	5·1	6·2
The tax system	12·7	7·0	9·9	6·4	5·1	8·6
International economy, trade, sterling	2·9	2·4	2·4	4·0	—	4·6
Manpower policies and unemployment	30·1	15·0	8·6	9·9	8·6	3·5
Public enterprise	12·7	5·1	3·5	2·9	3·5	2·4
Regional development	5·1	2·9	—	5·7	5·1	4·6
Industrial relations and industrial democracy	5·7	8·1	5·1	7·0	8·6	2·9
Policy on prices	9·9	14·5	12·1	9·9	7·5	7·0
Government support to industry	—	2·4	—	—	—	3·5
Consumer protection	—	—	—	—	—	2·9
Education	14·5	9·2	11·6	11·0	11·6	6·4
Social security, poverty and the means test	7·0	11·6	11·6	8·6	5·7	8·1
Welfare for whom?	2·9	2·4	5·1	5·7	2·9	3·5
Housing and rents	12·7	9·2	13·4	11·0	9·9	7·5
Participation and democracy	4·0	—	—	—	3·5	—
The mass media	—	—	—	2·9	—	2·4
The new environment	—	2·4	—	—	6·4	5·7
Overseas development	—	—	—	—	—	2·4
Military spending	—	2·4	—	2·4	—	2·9
European security	—	—	—	—	—	—
Commonwealth	—	—	—	—	—	—
Southern Africa	—	—	—	—	—	—
The United Nations	—	—	—	—	—	—

These omissions were criticised by many local parties. Five per cent of the replies took the opportunity to have a swipe at the Parliamentary Labour Party. Thus Thrapston: 'Unless the PLP is more directly guided by the mandates given by the Labour Party and TUC conferences, all activities, including this participation, can be considered as worthless.'

Nevertheless, the Labour leaders felt that on the whole the exercise had been useful in stimulating political discussion. 'Any scheme which gets 10,000 people involved in a serious discussion of the way the Labour Party is going cannot be a bad idea and the basic truth of this argument for the "participation" scheme should not be obscured by criticisms, however valid they may be.' Certainly the choice of priorities, which their heavy emphasis on economic and social policies (if not unexpected) is interesting in reflecting the current thinking within the party at the time the questions were put.

X

Europe — the great divide

The issue of Britain's entry into the European Economic Community produced one of the most bitter and divisive conflicts in the history of the Labour movement, as bitter and divisive as those over pacifism in the 1930s and unilateralism in the 1950s. It is true that the debate was conducted in a rather more civilised fashion, with less of the personal recriminations that marked the Bevanite clashes, when the issues were as much about personalities as policies. Nevertheless, the long-drawn-out wrangling over Europe threatened to prove as potentially damaging to Labour's chances, as the internecine feuds of the 1950s.

The Common Market question has been on the party scene for over twenty years. It was first raised with the publication of the Schuman Plan for Coal and Steel in 1950, which received scant support from the Attlee Government. Ernest Bevin, though fundamentally an internationalist, was lukewarm. When Kenneth Younger, then a junior Foreign Office Minister, tentatively suggested to his chief that there might be something to be said for Britain joining, Bevin cracked: 'Splash about young man, you'll learn to swim in time.'

It fell to the Tories, under Macmillan, to open serious negotiations with the EEC, but after months of talk in Brussels, in which Edward Heath first declared his passionate commitment to Europe, the negotiations foundered as a result of General de Gaulle's '*Non*' in January 1963.

Opinion both in the country and the main political parties was divided. Within the Labour Party, the main opposition came from the left, but included several prominent right-wingers, like Douglas Jay. Most people were content to adopt a 'wait and see' attitude. Hugh Gaitskell himself astounded the delegates, delighted the left and fell out with some of his closest associates at the Brighton party conference in 1962, when he made a speech amounting to outright hostility. British entry, he said, would mean 'the end of 1,000 years of British history' and would reduce us to the status of Texas or California. He laid down five conditions for acceptance:

1 Safeguarding the interests of the EFTA countries,
2 Maintaining Britain's right to plan its economy,
3 Protecting British agriculture,
4 Ensuring the right to an independent foreign policy, and
5 Safeguarding Commonwealth interests.

'If it is our conviction that the terms are not good enough, that we should not enter the Common Market on these terms, then the only right and proper and democratic thing is to let the people decide the issue,' he declared.

Europe was not a major election issue in 1964 or 1966. Labour's 1964 manifesto 'Time for decision' emphasised the need for safeguards – 'Labour believes that Britain, in consultation with her EFTA partners, should be ready to enter the EEC, provided essential British and Commonwealth interests are safeguarded.' The Conservatives in 1964 admitted that entry was a non-starter, but pledged themselves in 1966 to take the first favourable opportunity to apply for membership. Labour's line was expressed in 1966 by Harold Wilson in a speech at Bristol: 'Given a fair wind, we will negotiate our way into the Common Market, head held high, not crawl in.' Wilson himself had originally been against British entry, and in June 1962 expressed fears of 'the domination of West Europe by a Paris-Bonn axis dedicated to an intransigent line in East-West affairs, right-wing, possibly semi-neutralist and before long nuclear-powered'.

In the light of Labour's cautious and non-committal approach and the large element of hostility within the party, it came as a shock when in November 1966 Wilson announced the Government's intention of applying for membership of the EEC. Many different theories have been advanced to account for his conversion. One is that he wanted to keep George Brown, an ardent Marketeer, happy and in harness – Brown was said to have accepted the Foreign Secretaryship on condition that he was given his head over Europe. Another is that he relished the prospect of spiking Heath's guns. But the real reasons were undoubtedly the collapse of Labour's economic policies and the difficulties encountered in dealing with the Commonwealth and the USA. New policies and new alliances had become necessary and entry into Europe seemed to provide the answer.

Whatever his motives for the decision, Wilson made it clear that the Government was deadly serious. He told the House of Commons: 'I want the House, the country and our friends abroad to know that the Government are approaching the discussions I have foreshadowed with the clear intention and determination to enter EEC if, as we hope, our essential British and Commonwealth interests can be safeguarded. We mean business.'

In a speech to the Council of Europe at Strasbourg in January 1967 he said: 'The Government's purpose derives above all from our recognition that Europe is now faced with the opportunity of a great move forward in political unity and that we can, and indeed must, play our full part in it . . . This is an historic decision which could well determine the future of Britain, of Europe and indeed of the world for decades to come.' These were the words of a dedicated European – even George Brown or Roy Jenkins could hardly have expressed themselves more forcibly.

At that time the Cabinet was divided. The strongly pro-Europe faction included George Brown, Roy Jenkins, Tony Crosland, Ray Gunter and later Michael Stewart. The equally strongly anti-Europeans were Douglas Jay, Barbara Castle, Fred Peart and Anthony Greenwood. In between opinions were said to range from a cautiously 'pro' attitude of Wedgwood Benn, Patrick Gordon-Walker and Jim Callaghan to the slightly 'anti' position of Richard Crossman and Richard Marsh. On the whole, the Cabinet was prepared to give the project a chance and gave its blessing to the pilgrimage to Paris and other European capitals planned by Wilson and Brown in the winter of 1966-7.

The party conference in the autumn of 1967 endorsed the Government's decision to apply for membership.

For all the fine words and intensive campaigning the Wilson initiative collapsed. British entry was firmly and finally vetoed by De Gaulle in December – against the express wishes of the other Five Governments. After the General's fall from power in 1969 it became theoretically possible to revive negotiations, but there was no opportunity to press ahead with these before the General Election of 1970.

In the campaign, apart from the Liberals, the Scottish Nationalists and Enoch Powell, the Common Market issue featured very little. Butler and Pinto-Duchinsky (British General Election of 1970) estimated that 62 per cent of the Tory and 77 per cent of the Labour candidates made no reference to it in their election addresses. It was only after the election defeat, that Europe again became a live issue and opinion in the Labour movement began to swing against British entry. At the party conference in Blackpool in October 1970 an anti-Market resolution, moved by the Transport Workers' Union was only narrowly defeated – by 95,000 votes. The mover, Harry Urwin, claimed that the resolution was in line with public opinion – a current poll showed that only 22 per cent of the electorate supported British entry.

The NEC line was to reaffirm the 1969 position, which was to recommend entry, provided adequate safeguards were included for British and Commonwealth interests. Replying to the debate for the Executive, Joe Gormley the miners' President, said he respected the views of both the convinced opponents and supporters of British entry, but criticised those who had remained silent in the Cabinet and were now joining the anti-Market bandwagon. 'I do not think it is good enough for us to say that we should change our policy on such important issues just because we do not happen to be in government,' he said.

The Government's terms of entry were published in a White Paper in July 1971. On 17 July the Labour Party held a special conference – the first special conference since 1918 when the issue was whether to stay in Lloyd-George's Coalition Government. Ian Mikardo in the chair was scrupulously fair in calling alternatively on pro- and anti-Marketeers, and the debate was conducted on a hard-hitting, but non-abusive level. The fact that no vote was taken led Hugh Scanlon to describe the conference as 'an exercise in futility' but both pro- and anti-Marketeers were reasonably satisfied at the outcome.

The discussion centred on the issue of the acceptability of the terms negotiated by the Heath Government. George Thomson, who was Labour's Minister specially concerned with Europe, declared categorically that had Labour won the election he would have recommended the Government to accept the terms, and that this view was shared by most of those who had been involved in the negotiations. (Michael Stewart, George Brown and Lord Chalfont were all known to take this view.) 'The terms that have come out are not ideal,' said Thomson. 'None of us ever believed in the Labour Government that ideal terms would come ... My personal judgement is that if we had won the Election and had still been facing the realities, the responsibilities and limitations of government, these terms would have gone through a Labour Cabinet.' He appealed to the movement to agree to disagree and preserve party unity in order to concentrate on getting the Tories out.

Speakers on both sides veered between economics and emotionalism. 'We mustn't let down our comrades in Europe,' said the Market supporters. 'The people of Britain must decide,' countered the anti-Market men.

Peter Shore, a consistent opponent, warned: 'The terms are appallingly bad for the people of this country ... We are in for a great national disaster if we are to enter on these terms.'

Jack Jones, TGWU, said that only four out of 900 delegates at his union's annual conference were in favour of entry, but Fred Hayday, General and Municipal Workers, said that his union thought the terms were acceptable. Clive Jenkins, Managerial Staffs, conjured up the image of 'a distant Brussels bureaucracy dominated by the great companies', but Jack Peel, (Dyers, Bleachers and Textile Workers): 'We believe we have a better chance inside the market of improving the living standards of those we represent.'

Harold Wilson, winding up the debate, repeated his conditions of entry: a reduction in the burden on Britain's balance of payments; safeguards against speculative movements of capital; safeguards for the interests of Commonwealth sugar producers and special treatment for New Zealand producers. Wilson insisted that he had been consistent in his attitude: 'I reject the assertions, wherever they come from, that the terms this Conservative Government have obtained are the terms the Labour Government asked for, the terms the Labour Government would have asked for, the terms the Labour Government would have been bound to accept. I reject these assertions.' Finally, he appealed for tolerance and mutual respect: 'We must recognise that what divides us is an important policy issue, not an article of faith.'

The arguments for and against entry were to be repeated on both sides, at subsequent meetings, conferences and debates, and it would be both unnecessary and tedious to recall them in detail. The only significant development after the special conference was a change in atmosphere. As the hard-line anti-Marketeers grew tougher and more confident, so the pro-Marketeers became increasingly dispirited and defeatist. They had done their conference arithmetic and knew that they were overwhelmingly beaten.

At Brighton in October 1971 conference carried by a five to one majority a NEC resolution, opposing entry on Conservative terms, demanding a General Election and calling on all MPs to vote against the Government in the forthcoming House of Commons debate. This was underlined by Callaghan: 'It is our job on 28 October to get the Tories out. And therefore we need the maximum vote on that day. The National Executive judges that the mood of the party is that all members of the party should join hands on this issue and accept the verdict of the party.'

Despite the conference decision and Callaghan's statement, no fewer than sixty-nine Labour MPs defied the Whip and voted with the Government on the principle of entry, when the fateful day arrived. No fewer than twenty abstained. The rebels invoked a Clause in Standing Orders which substituted the words 'deeply held personal convictions' for the original 'conscience' clause to justify their action.

This change had been initiated in 1968 by Douglas Houghton, chairman of the PLP. Houghton wrote later (*The Parliamentarian*, January 1972) that it brought dissent from the official party line on the EEC within the protection of "deeply held personal conviction'.

On the Conservative side thirty-nine MPs voted against the Government and three abstained. The final vote was 356 to 244.

At its first meeting after the debate the NEC called on all MPs to oppose the detailed EEC legislation: 'Party unity and the possibility of an early replacement of the Conservative Government demand a full response to Party policy by all Labour MP's. The majority of Marketeers having made their position clear on the matter of principle agreed to fall in with this requirement. A handful of Labour MPs continued to abstain. The Bill went through ninety-six divisions, in some of which the Government only just scraped home. The majority for the second reading was eight and on one committee stage amendment, tabled by the strange alliance of Messrs Powell, Foot, Walker-Smith and Shore, the majority was down to five. The Bill had its Third Reading on 13 July and was given the Royal Assent on 17 October 1972.

In spite of his conduct on 28 October 1971 and a warning from the *New Statesman* that his re-election would be 'disastrous', Roy Jenkins had retained the deputy leadership in the November Parliamentary party elections, with a majority of fourteen over Michael Foot. The balance in the Shadow Cabinet remained substantially the same, with three ardent Marketeers – Shirley Williams, George Thomson and Harold Lever – countered by two equally ardent opponents, Michael Foot and Peter Shore, who were appointed Labour spokesmen on Europe. Douglas Houghton had a majority of only seven against Norman Pentland for the chairmanship.

Despite the presence of these allies Jenkins began to find his position increasingly uncomfortable. 'Shades of the prison-house began to close about the growing Roy.' The last straw was the NEC decision to back Wedgwood Benn's plan for a referendum. This had been turned down at the party conference, but the NEC voted thirteen to eleven in its favour and its example was followed by the Shadow Cabinet. Jenkins wrote to Wilson (9 April) that this was only 'a single incident illustrating and accentuating a growing divergence', and that opposition to the terms of entry was increasingly becoming one of opposition on principle. 'I want to see the present Government replaced by a Labour Government, but I also want to see that future Labour Governments have a clear sense of direction ... If Government is born out of opportunism it becomes not merely difficult but impossible .. The constant shifting of ground I cannot accept.'

George Thomson and Harold Lever resigned along with Jenkins. Their places were filled by Reg Prentice and John Silkin, while Barbara Castle replaced Edward Short, who became deputy leader.

Roy Jenkins was not a 'hail-fellow well-met' type and did not fit easily into the House tea-room atmosphere. Some of his supporters gave the impression of intellectual arrogance and just as the Gaitskellites were accused of being an esoteric Hampstead set, so the Jenkinsites were regarded by the Left as elitist, without any roots in the wider movement. Only a handful of trade union leaders backed British entry – Tom Bradley (TSSA) Jack Peel (dyers) Roy Grantham (APEX) and Lord Cooper (GMWU). Some like Joe Gormley (miners) and Jim Conway (engineers) supported the EEC as individuals, but were bound by their union policies to oppose it. The most powerful union leaders, like Jack Jones and Hugh Scanlon, were consistent in their opposition. The pro-Marketeers' main outside organisation is the Labour Committee for Europe, but it consists mainly of MPs and peers, and until the appointment of Jim Cattermole, former East Midlands regional organiser, made little effort to enlist a wider following. By contrast, the Labour Committee for Safeguards, with Douglas Jay as its chairman and Ron Leighton as secretary, organised rallies, meetings and grass-roots propaganda in constituencies and trade union branches.

The next stage in the long drawn-out Common Market battle was the rejection of British entry by the TUC at its September 1972 conference. The anti-Marketeers confidently expected that the party conference would follow suit, and it very nearly did. An AEUW resolution of outright opposition was only narrowly defeated, after a recount, at the Blackpool conference in October. The narrowness of the margin did not detract from the relief of the pro-Marketeers, who had had a rough ride during the debate. Roy Jenkins said later: 'It could have been a great deal worse.' The anti-Marketeers were equally jubilant at the overwhelming defeat of a pro-European resolution and at the success of the Boilermakers' composite motion, which was more subtly anti-European than that of the AUEW. It proposed even tougher terms of entry than those put forward by the NEC and called for a boycott of all the ECC institutions, including the European Parliament 'until the assent of the British electorate has been given'.

The NEC's own statement, carried by a three to one majority, reiterated Labour's opposition to entry on the present terms, committed a future Labour Government to re-negotiate these and repeated the call for a referendum. 'If these two tests are passed – a successful renegotiation and the expressed approval of the majority of the people, then we shall be ready to play our full part in developing a new and wider Europe. If negotiations do not succeed, we shall not regard the Treaty obligations as binding upon us.'

The drafting of this statement and his speech introducing it were hailed as a tactical success for Wilson, who was determined to preserve party unity at any price, and retain a free hand for a future Labour Government. It was in order not to jeopardise Wilson's move that Roy Jenkins decided not to take part in the debate. He realised that Wilson had protected him and his followers from the full fury of the left on more than one occasion. Many members of the Tribune group resented the kid-glove treatment accorded to the Jenkinsites, comparing it with the harsh discipline formerly meted out to the Bevanites. But Michael Foot, who had been elected top of the constituency section of the NEC and given a standing conference ovation, advocated tolerance. He told an anti-Market rally at Blackpool: 'I am not proposing to be a party to stamping out the rights of the minority ... I did not come to this conference to help drive Roy Jenkins out of the party. I came to this conference to try to drive Ted Heath out of Ten Downing Street.'

The upshot of the Blackpool conference was that the party was left facing two ways, instead of the three which would have been the case had the AEUW motion been carried. But the passage of the Boilermakers' boycott resolution put the PLP in a dilemma, when it had to decide whether to send a delegation to the Strasbourg Parliament of Europe. On 13 December, following a typical compromise adopted by the Shadow Cabinet, it decided by 140 votes to 55 to adopt delaying tactics and to wait for a year. The minority was smaller than that which had voted with the Government on 28 October 1971, but an amendment moved by George Cunningham secured 88 votes against 134. This suggested that Labour should participate 'in order to moderate the adverse consequences of membership of the Community during Conservative Government'. Though himself an anti-Marketeer, Cunningham recognised the realities of the situation after 1 January 1973.

The PLP decision had a very bad press both in Britain and Europe. Socialist leaders on the Continent were dismayed at the vote which, according to the Dutch Foreign Minister, had robbed the socialist group of the chance of becoming 'the strongest pressure group in Europe'. George Thomson, appointed as one of the two British EEC Commissioners, said that European socialists found it 'a bitter and bewildering disappointment'. 'By the time of the next General Election British integration in the Community will have proceeded so far that British membership will be an established fact of life ... It will make electoral nonsense to appear to wish to wreck it ... Political parties, if they wish to be supported by the electorate, have to come to terms with reality.'

With entry into the EEC a *fait accompli* there were hopes that the storm and fury over British entry into Europe would die down, despite the continued pressure from the anti-Marketeers. It is difficult to imagine that once, in, a Labour Government, especially if still led by Harold Wilson, could, or would, take Britain out of Europe.

XI

What Labour stands for

Morgan Phillips told a meeting of the Socialist International in Amsterdam: 'The British Labour Party is Methodist, not Marxist.' (This statement, reported by Ian Mackay, made the splash headline in the *News Chronicle*, such were news values in the late 1940s). The remark was true, in the sense that there has always been a strong streak of nonconformity in the Labour movement, particularly in the Welsh valleys, where loyalty to the party burns fiercely. Labour has also always chosen the path of evolution rather than revolution and upheld the democratic processes. Morgan Phillips' statement, however, does not by itself add up to a philosophy of social-democracy, nor was it meant to.

Here we come back to Crosland's question: 'What do we stand for now?' Many people have for years sought to define the nature of British socialism. The exercise is really extremely difficult because there are so many different strands in the make-up of the movement and so many conflicting ideas. Labour as has been shown is a coalition of varying interests and opinions and there are perpetual shifts in the internal balance of power.

In the 1940s and 1950s, the right wing was on top. By the 1970s the left wing was dominant in the National Executive, the trade unions and the constituency parties, though not in the Parliamentary party where the centre still held the balance. The dominance of the left was exemplified by the decision at the 1972 Blackpool conference to re-affirm its faith in Clause Four. (The text of this, the public ownership clause, is given on p. 41.) A resolution was adopted declaring 'This conference instructs the next Labour Government to implement Clause Four in full ... it believes that this is imperative for the survival of the Labour Party and the future of Socialism.'

Ian Mikardo, replying for the NEC, said: 'Today Clause Four is not just a theory and an aspiration. It is the only basis on which we can put new spirit and vigour into our economic life,' adding, 'We are all Clause Four men now.'

Thirteen years earlier, in the same hall, Hugh Gaitskell had dared to challenge the Ark of the Covenant and question the relevance of Clause 4 to the needs of socialism in the sixties. 'It seems to me that this needs to be brought up to date,' he said. 'It implies that common ownership is an end, whereas in fact it is a means.' 'It implies that we propose to nationalise everything, but do we? Of course not. I am sure that the Webbs and Arthur Henderson who largely drafted this Constitution would have been amazed and horrified had they thought that their words were to be treated as sacrosanct forty years later. Let us remember that we are a party of the future, not of the past ... It is no good waving the banners of a bygone age.'

Gaitskell's speech aroused bitter resentment, especially his statement that nationalisation had, on balance, lost the party votes in the 1959 election. The conflict rumbled on for some time before it was submerged in the even more controversial and divisive argument about unilateralism. Expressing the left-wing union point of view Frank Cousins said in March 1960: 'If some of the elite of the party can define it (Clause Four) as saying that it will be kept in to satisfy the fuddy-duddies and sentimentalists of the unions, we in our union will be proud to join the ranks of the sentimentalists and fuddy-duddies, because we are proud of our belief in Clause Four.'

Benn Levy, the playwright and former MP, spoke for the left in the constituency parties when he said it was not nationalisation that had lost votes, but the leadership's 'ambiguous and apologetic attitude towards it' and the 'soft-pedalling' of socialist faith and beliefs. 'I believe firmly that this kind of behaviour of half-heartedness which has been nicknamed Butskellism (a term coined by the *Economist* to describe the identity between Gaitskell and R. A. Butler) has done serious damage, has made our public image ineffectual and has greatly injured the dynamic strength of our party.'

In the end the NEC adopted a statement of aims designed to complement and explain Clause 4. It contained twelve points, all lofty and high-minded. The salient one in the Clause 4 debate was No. 10 which stated that the party's economic and social objectives 'can be achieved only through an expansion of common ownership substantial enough to give the community power over the commanding heights of the economy'. (This was Nye Bevan's famous compromise phrase which has passed into the party's language, along with many other of his sayings.) The statement also recognised that both public and private enterprise had a place in the economy.

This declaration was made in 1960. Since then, despite two Labour Governments, there has been only one major act of nationalisation – that of steel. A plan to take over the docks was cut short by the 1970 election. There was no attempt to change the original Morrisonian concept of public ownership through huge State corporations, which were not directly accountable to Parliament although this method of nationalisation had been criticised by many Labour MPs.

The Clause 4 row of 1959 is past history now. Nobody since Gaitskell has had the temerity publicly to raise the possibility of bringing it up to date. But the bitterness and hostility he aroused through his tentative and many thought ill-timed, proposal suggests that difficulties in finding a policy over common ownership which will accommodate both the left and the right wings are by no means resolved.

Harold Wilson, like Gaitskell, took as his main text the need for change when he addressed the 1963 conference – his first as party leader. Unlike Gaitskell he took care not to tread on any traditional toes but developed a new theme – the need for the party to adapt itself to the changing technological society. 'In all our plans,' he said, 'we are re-defining and we are re-stating our socialism in terms of the scientific revolution. But that revolution cannot become a reality unless we are prepared to make far-reaching changes in economic and social attitudes which permeate our whole system of society.'

Ten years later Wilson adopted a new policy theme – the need to protect the individual against the 'soulless' nature of modern capitalist society. His speeches at Edinburgh and Newcastle in the early months of 1973 were important not just because, as we have seen, they brought the old Wilson back to life, but because, after a long period of doing little but Tory-bashing, he set a new emphasis on a cause which has always been near to Labour's heart. In 1969 the NEC adopted a propaganda campaign under the title 'Labour's got life and soul', designed to emphasise the party's compassion and humanity. Some people accused Wilson of stealing Anthony Wedgwood Benn's clothes; others pointed out that he had not only captured the Tory philosophy of 'Set the people free', which had been their battle-cry from 1950 onwards, but also the Liberals' slogan 'People count'.

At Edinburgh, with an array of words which would defy a Thesaurus, he attacked the 'free market vandalism of the barons of the multi-national mega-corporations'. 'A people drilled, dragooned and distracted into believing that there is no choice, that they are denied any real power to choose, can find themselves drifting into a target for extremists. This is the danger, as democrats, that we could face in Britain. The danger . . . that we could see a lurch into Fascism.'

Labour has often been regarded as a party of bureaucrats who believe in the dictum that 'The man in Whitehall knows best.' Wilson at Newcastle concentrated his fire on Whitehall bureaucracy and Heath's tendency to transfer local authority functions to Government-appointed bodies. 'People say that they do not know what is going on, or why, and that whatever it is, they have no say in it.'

The National Executive presented to the 1972 conference a lengthy omnibus 'Programme for Britain' which, it stressed, was a document for discussion and not an election manifesto. It covers a vast range of subjects and would take many years of Parliamentary time to meet in full, as well as vastly increased public spending. Most of the subjects were being studied in depth during 1972–3 by a series of working parties and expert groups set up by the NEC to form the basis of a future election manifesto.

The job of actually drawing up the manifesto falls to the

NEC, jointly with the Parliamentary Labour Party, on the basis of the programme agreed by the party conference passed by a two-thirds majority. It is up to the two elected bodies to decide on priorities. This is explicitly laid down in Clause 5 of the Constitution. It is ironic that the group which wants to diminish the powers of the PLP seems sometimes conveniently to forget this clause!

Wilson, in his Edinburgh speech, listed his own choice of priorities, which seem to make good electoral sense. These are in four main areas:

1 *Housing*; measures to eliminate profiteering in private housing, with increased powers for local authorities to purchase privately rented property and handle all unfurnished rented accommodation; repeal of the Housing Finance Act; protection of tenants against eviction; the doubling of rating values to enforce the use of empty office blocks, e.g. Centre Point.

2 *Nationalisation of building land:* with a 'comprehensive, socialist and irreversible' policy. Land nationalisation has been one of Labour's objectives since the party was born, but, apart from the rather timid experiment with the Land Commission in 1966 it has never reached the Statute book. 'God gave the land to the people' could be an election winner, at a time when the public is disgusted with rocketing land values and astronomic house-buying costs.

3 *North sea oil*: plans to ensure that the benefits of the exploitation of North sea gas and oil accrue to the nation.

4 *Transport;* to be free or low-cost in London and other big conurbations; plans to step up investment in the railways and divert to them much traffic from the roads.

The Labour Party is, of course, already committed to the repeal of the Industrial Relations Act and plans for taking over banks and insurance institutions were well advanced in the spring of 1973. The idea of a State holding agency on the lines of the Italian agency IRI has been put forward.

Many people believe that Labour would be ill-advised to tie itself up too closely to a specific programme or introduce a 'shopping list'. This is the view of Anthony Crosland, one of the party's intellectuals. In *The Observer* (21 January 1973) he wrote: 'The detailed policies which we are gradually acquiring do not appear to be informed by a coherent vision of the society we want to see. Last year's programmes (contained in "Programme for Britain") seemed rather a collection of bits and pieces with more emphasis on means than ends ... It was not always clear what this flurry of activity was intended to achieve, nor why it should be more effective than the similar flurry after 1964.'

Crosland aligned himself with the philosophies of Gaitskell and Roy Jenkins in placing the main emphasis on creating a more egalitarian society. 'The essential socialist objectives are greater equality and a more classless society – these should be the central theme of any Labour manifesto ... Gross economic inequalities remain and have been made worse by Mr Heath, and socially we remain the most class-ridden country in the world.' His solution: 'bash the rich' measures with a wealth tax, a gifts tax, and the public ownership of land, 'to communicate to the country a clear vision of a fairer and more equal Britain'.

A greater sharing out of wealth between the rich and the poor, and greater equality of opportunity, particularly for minorities, such as women and immigrants, should be the cornerstone of future Labour policy. As Hugh Gaitskell put it, Labour must be a party of 'conscience and reform'.

It is doubtful, in any case, how far detailed election manifestos influence public opinion, any more than do candidates' election addresses. People have become increasingly mistrustful of politicians and their election pledges. This began under the Labour Government and developed into widespread cynicism as a result of the Conservatives' broken promises and somersaults. What the public want to know, broadly, is what a political party stands for and whether it can provide good government.

I

Joe Gormley, the miners' President, said in a debate on the results of the 1970 election: 'One thing which a great political party needs is to be seen to be credible, responsible and consistent.' And in the same vein Roy Jenkins[1] said: 'When the next election comes, we shall not be judged by the vehemence of our perorations, still less by the dexterity with which we follow the transient twists and turns of public opinion. We shall be judged by the quality of the programme we put before our fellow-citizens, and by the consistency and courage with which we advocate it.'

The future for Labour depends upon a number of imponderable factors. Some are short-term and related to immediate election tactics. For example, can the party come to terms with the unions and work out a viable system for tackling inflation and improving industrial relations? Can it re-unite its ranks and heal the breaches created by the European issue? Can it improve its machinery and organisation and maintain the morale of its workers and supporters?

On a longer-term and more philosophical plane, can Labour achieve its objectives of creating a fairer and juster society, while at the same time safeguarding personal liberties and extending the sense of participation? Can it offer policies which are recognised as being relevant to the needs of the mid-1970s and not a hangover from the past? Above all, can it persuade the electorate that its leaders have courage and consistency? This is perhaps the only way to counter public cynicism and disillusionment about political parties.

Elections are won by appealing to the broad mass of the voters and by convincing them that the party is fit to govern. It is not enough to produce dogma which satisfy the faithful. The public is not all that interested in the semantics of socialism, nor in the complexities of Clauses 4 and 5 of the constitution.

Labour's dilemma is that if it is to achieve power, it must broaden the basis of its appeal, even at the risk of alienating those groups whose sole interest lies in protest-making. It must continue to operate as a coalition.

[1] Roy Jenkins, *What Matters Now* (Collins/Fontana 1972).

XII

Postscript

The scene: The Winter Gardens, Blackpool. The date: 5 October 1973. The Occasion: the closing session of the Labour Party conference ending, traditionally, with the singing of the Red Flag. The leaders on the platform and the delegates in the emptying (Friday morning) hall sang the words as if they meant them, as well as actually knowing them. During their four-day conference, which many believed could be the last before the general election, they had 'raised the scarlet standard high'. They had re-enshrined Clause Four, in all its purity, as the centre-piece of socialist philosophy. They had accorded to Harold Wilson a standing ovation and confirmed his unchallenged authority as Leader. They had declared to the world that a united party, beating off the Liberal challenge, would fight, and win, the next election on a socialist programme – and the next election after that. Above all, Blackpool 1973 had given fresh evidence of what Aneurin Bevan once called the party's 'passion for unity'.

Moderates like Shirley Williams and Denis Healey had been elected to the National Executive, along with left-wingers Ian Mikardo and Lena Jeger. Roy Jenkins had been given a courteous hearing and the conference as a whole clearly accepted Michael Foot's impassioned plea for tolerance: 'Our part is a democratic party, not a totalitarian party.'

Michael Foot also scored a tactical success in the private session when he persuaded delegates not to accept a resolution which would have bound MPs to accept conference decisions or else risk being refused endorsement.

Later in the month, an equal desire for unity and for the cohesion of the coalition was reflected in the voting for the

Shadow Cabinet. Roy Jenkins, after his self-imposed exile on the back benches, was returned with a respectable vote of 144, only six less than the vote cast for James Callaghan, who topped the poll. Fred Peart, Labour's spokesman on defence, lost his seat. The voting results showed a healthy balance between right and left, pro- and anti-market forces.

J. Callaghan	150
M. Foot	147
R. Prentice	146
A. Crosland	145
R. Jenkins	144
Mrs S. Williams	138
D. Healey	129
A. Benn	110
H. Lever	110
M. Rees	108
P. Shore	104
W. Ross	99

From the points of view of raising morale and stimulating enthusiasm, the 1973 conference was a tremendous success. There had been nothing like it since 1945 – indeed it was significant how many speakers harked nostalgically to the achievements of the Attlee Government and how little relatively was said about the problems of the Wilson Governments, in the face of economic and financial crisis. Next time, Tony Wedgwood Benn assured delegates, 'The crisis that we inherit when we come to power will be the occasion for fundamental change, not the excuse for postponing it'. Delegates relished the prospect of meeting the challenge of capitalist power, whether in industry, the City or the mass media.

Some warning notes were sounded. Thus Roy Jenkins: 'Let us be radical by all means, but let us be responsible and rational as well . . . We need to promise no more than we are convinced we can do.' He added pointedly that it was a mistake to think of the election as already won. The polls showed only a 38 per cent Labour voting intention. (Later in the week an opinion poll put the Labour voting intention at 34 per cent, with the Liberals second at 32 per cent and the Tories third at 31 per cent.

Shirley Williams, at a Socialist Commentary tea-party, wondered whether it was wise to concentrate so much on public ownership, which was not a priority in the minds of the electors. Unless the gap between electors and party activists were bridged, they would play into the hands of the Liberals and people like Dick Taverne.

Harold Wilson likewise warned: 'We are debating not what we would like to do if we had political power; we are debating what we must do to turn our debates into the reality of political power. Otherwise the party will be reduced for years to the frustrations of parliamentary opposition.'

Wilson, in introducing Labour's Programme 1973 had presented the most formidable agenda for public ownership for many years. His list comprised: land required for development, redevelopment and improvement up to the end of the century; the mineral wealth underground; North Sea gas and oil; all ports and docks; shipbuilding and ancillary industries; the aircraft industry; sections or firms in the pharmaceutical, machine-tool, construction and road haulage industries. A new Industry Act would empower the Government to issue directives to firms about prices, profits, investments, overseas trade and industrial relations and to purchase individual companies, all the powers being applicable to multinational companies operating in Britain. A National Enterprise Board would be set up with power to take a controlling interest in relevant companies in profitable manufacturing industries. Banking and insurance were still under consideration, as was a proposal for a State merchant bank.

Wilson refused to accept the commitment to take over twenty-five leading companies, which had caused such a furore in June, and the conference accepted his advice by throwing out, by 5,600,000 votes to 291,000, a motion re-affirming this commitment.

The programme, he insisted, was 'realistic, radical and relevant'. They were not dealing with hard-faced individuals of pre-war capitalism, but with 'increasingly anonymous, unidentifiable, often faceless, more often soulless corporations, national and multi-national'. 'To be relevant as Clem Attlee's Government was relevant, we have to be bold enough to deal with a totally new dimension.' In addition, they had to 'socialise' the industries which Attlee had nationalised and inject real industrial democracy into them.

Other proposals approved by conference included raising old age pensions, eliminating private practice and prescription charges from the National Health Service and building more houses. Labour is also committed to repealing such unpopular Tory measures as the Industrial Relations Act, and the Housing Finance Act, and to re-negotiating the terms of entry into the European Economic Community, followed by a vote of the British people. Another 'top' priority is the control of prices, especially food prices, but the thorny question of incomes policy is being left to talks between party and TUC leaders.

And to pay for this massive programme? Denis Healey, Shadow Chancellor, announced that there would have to be swinging measures of taxation, with higher taxes on incomes above about £4,000 a year. 'A lot of you will pay extra tax. That goes particularly for every MP in this hall, including me. If we really believe in greater equality, we must be prepared to make sacrifices ourselves.' Healey's warning may have been realistic, but many delegates feared that he might have saddled them with an electoral albatross. As *The Times* commentator wrote: 'The gloom in the conference hall at this announcement could have been cut with a knife.'

No votes were taken on the document Programme for Britain, and it will now fall to the National Executive and the Shadow Cabinet jointly to draw up an election manifesto from the wide-ranging proposals and to select the topmost priorities from the many priorities which were named top. There will clearly be tensions between those who counsel moderation and those who want to go all the way with conference. Any thoughts that the radical nature of the programme could be watered down or selectivity carried too far would meet with bitter opposition from the left, which stands for the unimpaired authority of party conference.

Harold Wilson in the autumn of 1973 embarked on a deliberate gamble. He evidently decided that the most important consideration was to mobilise the support and enthusiasm of active party workers and trade unionists, in presenting a radical socialist programme, rather than to trim any sails to win middle-class and floating voters. He dismissed the Liberals with contempt and pledged that in no circumstances would he enter into any coalition or alliance. But concern about the Liberal advance in by-elections and opinion polls was evident by the considerable time he devoted to pouring scorn on their inconsistency and irrelevance – a case of 'the lady doth protest too much, methinks?'

It has been said that Edward Heath risked a gamble with the British economy in his Stage Three anti-inflation proposals. To my mind, Wilson's political gamble is on a far bigger scale. If Labour loses the next election, party members can at least have the satisfaction of knowing they stuck to their principles. But defeat would be the signal for a new bout of feuding and recrimination and would certainly undermine Wilson's own position. If Labour wins – and in the autumn of 1973 the unpopularity of the Tories led many people to believe that it would – then it has an unparalleled chance to show that it can be a party of protest *and* power. In the meantime, the question mark in the title of this book must remain.

Appendixes

APPENDIX I

Labour Party membership, 1900–1971

	Constituency and Central Parties No.	Total Individual Membership		Trade Unions		Socialist and Co-operative Societies, etc.		* Total Membership
		Men	Women	No.	Membership	No.	Membership	
1900	7	—	—	41	353,070	3	22,861	375,931
1901	21	—	—	65	455,450	2	13,861	469,311
1902	49	—	—	127	847,315	2	13,835	861,150
1903	76	—	—	165	965,025	2	13,775	969,800
1904	73	—	—	158	855,270	2	14,730	900,000
1905	73	—	—	158	904,496	2	16,784	921,280
1906	83	—	—	176	975,182	2	20,855	998 338
1907	92	—	—	181	1,049,673	2	22,267	1,072,413
1908	133	—	—	176	1,127,035	2	27,465	1,158,565
1909	155	—	—	172	11450,648	2	30,982	1,486,308
1910	148	—	—	151	1,394,403	2	31,377	1,430,539
1911	149	—	—	141	1,501,783	2	31,404	1,539,092
1912	146	—	—	130	1,858,178	2	311237	1,895,498
1913	158	—	—	†	†	2	33,304	†
1914	179	—	—	101	1,572,391	2	33,230	1,612,147
1915	177	—	—	111	2,053,735	2	32,828	2,093,365
1916	199	—	—	119	2,170,782	3	42,190	2,219,764
1917	239	—	—	123	2,415,383	3	47,140	2,465,131
1918	389	—	—	131	2,960,409	4	52,720	3,013,129
1919	418	—	—	126	3,464,020	7	47,270	3,511,290
1920	492	—	—	122	4,317,537	5	42,270	4,359,807
1921	456	—	—	116	3,973,558	5	36,803	4,010,361
1922	482	—	—	102	3,279,276	5	31,760	3,311,036
1923	503	—	—	106	3,120,149	6	35,762	3,155,911
1924	529	—	—	108	3,158,002	7	36,397	3,194,399
1925	549	—	—	106	3,337,635	8	36,235	3,373,870
1926	551	—	—	104	3,352,347	8	35,939	3,388,286
1927	532	—	—	97	3,238,939	6	54,676	3,293,615
1928	535	214,970		91	2,025,139	7	52,060‡	2,292,169
1929	578	227,897		91	2,044,279	6	58,669‡	2,330,845
1930	607	277,211		89	2,011,484	7	58,213‡	2,346,908
1931	608	297,003		80	2,024,216	7	36,847‡	2,358,066
1932	608	371,607		75	1,906,269	9	39,911‡	2,371,787
1933	612	211,223	154,790	75	1,899,007	9	40,010‡	2,305,030
1934	614	222,777	158,482	72	1,857,524	8	39,707‡	2,278,490
1935	614	246,401	172,910	72	1,912,924	9	45,280‡	2,377,515
1936	614	250,761	179,933	73	1,968,538	9	45,125‡	2,444,357
1937	614	258,060	189,090	70	2,037,071	8	43,451‡	2,527,672
1938	614	250,705	178,121	70	2,158,076	9	43,384‡	2,630,286
1939	614	239.978	168,866	72	2,214,070	6	40,153‡	2,663,067
1940	614	175,606	128,518	73	2,226,575	6	40,464‡	2,571,163
1941	585	129,909	96,713	68	2,230,728	6	28,108‡	2,485,458
1942	581	123,101	95,682	69	2,206,209	6	28,940‡	2,453,932

Labour Party membership, 1900–1971 (continued)

	Constituency and Central Parties No.	Total Individual Membership Men	Total Individual Membership Women	Trade Unions No.	Trade Unions Membership	Socialist and Co-operative Societies, etc. No.	Socialist and Co-operative Societies, etc. Membership	* Total Membership
1943	586	134,697	100,804	69	2,237,307	6	30,432‡	2,503,240
1944	598	153,132	112,631	68	2 375,381	6	31,701‡	2,672,845
1945	649	291,435	195,612	69	2,510,369	6	41,281‡	3,038,697
1946	649	384,023	261,322	70	2,635,346	6	41,667‡	3,322,358
1947	649	361,643	246,844	73	4,386,074	6	45,738‡	5,040,299
1948	656	375,861	253,164	80	4,751,030	6	42,382‡	5,422,437
1949	660	439,591	290,033	80	4,946,207	5	41,116‡	5,716,947
1950	661	543,434	364,727	83	4,971,911	5	40,100‡	5,920,172
1951	667	512,751	363,524	82	4,937,427	5	35,300‡	5,849,002
1952	667	594,663	419,861	84	5,071,935	5	21,200‡	6,107,659
1953	667	584,626	420,059	84	5,056,912	5	34,425‡	6,096,022
1954	667	544,042	389,615	84	5,529,760	5	34,610‡	6,498,027
1955	667	488,687	354,669	87	5,605,988	5	34,650‡	6,483,994
1956	667	489,735	355,394	88	5,658,249	5	33,850‡	6,537,228
1957	667	527,787	385,200	87	5,644,012	5	25,550‡	6,582,549
1958	667	515,298	373,657	87	5,627,690	5	25,541‡	6,542,186
1959	667	492,213	355,313	87	5,564,010	5	25,450‡	6,436,986
1960	667	459,584	330,608	86	5,512,688	5	25,450‡	6,328,330
1961	667	434,511	316,054	86	5,549,592	5	25,450‡	6,325,607
1962	667	444,576	322,883	86	5,502,773	5	25,475‡	6,295,707
1963	667	480,639	349,707	83	5,507,232	6	20,858‡	6,358,436
1964	667	478,910	351,206	81	5,502,001	6	21,200‡	6,353,317
1965	659	475,164	341,601	79	5,601,982	6	21,146‡	6.439,893
1966	658	454,722	320,971	79	5,538,744	6	21,175‡	6,335,612
1967	657	427,495	306,437	75	5,539,562	6	21,120‡	6,294,614
1968	656	401,499	299,357	68	5,364,484	6	21,285‡	6,086,625
1969	656	387,856	292,800	68	5,461,721	6	21,505‡	6,163,882
1970	656	394,290	285,901	67	5,518,520	6	23,869‡	6,222,580
1971	659	699,522		67	5,559,371	6	25,360	6,284,253

* The totals to 1917 in this column include the membership of the Co-operative and Women's Labour League affiliations, in addition to those of the Trade Unions and the Socialist Societies.

† Owing to the operation of the Osborne Judgment it was impossible to compile membership statistics for 1913.

‡ The Royal Arsenal Co-operative Society, through its Political Purposes Committee, continues its affilation with the Party, and its membership is included in these totals.

Source: Labour Party Annual Report 1972.

APPENDIX II

General Elections, 1900–1970

Year	Electorate	% Poll	Labour Candi-dates	Labour Members elected	Labour Vote
1900	6,730,935	74·6	15	2	62,698
1906	7,264,608	82·6	50	29	323,195
1910 (Jan)	7,694,741	86·6	78	40	505,690
1910 (Dec)	7,709,981	81·1	56	42	370,802
1918	21,392,322	57·2	361	57	2,245,777
1922	20,874,456	73·0	414	142	4,237,349
1923	21,283,061	71·1	427	191	4,439,780
1924	21,730,988	77·0	514	151	5,489,087
1929	28,854,748	76·3	569	289	8,370,417
1931†	29,952,361	76·4	491	46	6,324,737
1935	31,374,449	71·1	552	154	8,325,491
1945†	33,240,391	72·8	603	393	11,967,746
1950†	34,412,255	83·9	617	315	13,266,176
1951†	34,919,331	82·6	617	295	13,948,883
1955†	34,852,179	76·8	620	277	12,405,254
1959†	35,397,304	78·7	621	258	12,216,172
1964†	35,894,054	77·1	628	317	12,205,808
1966†	35,957,245	75·8	621*	363*	13,066,166*
1970†	39,342,013	72·0	624*	287*	12,179,341*

† includes Northern Ireland Labour.
* excluding the Speaker.

Source: Labour Party Diary 1973.

APPENDIX III

1906–8	J. Keir Hardie
1908–10	Arthur Henderson
1910–11	George Barnes
1911–14	J. Ramsay MacDonald
1914–17	Arthur Henderson
1917–21	W. Adamson
1921–2	J. R. Clynes

CHAIRMEN AND LEADERS

1922–31	J. Ramsay MacDonald
1931–2	Arthur Henderson
1932–5	George Lansbury
1935–55	C. R. Attlee
1955–63	Hugh Gaitskell
1963–	Harold Wilson

PARTY SECRETARIES

1900–12	J. Ramsay MacDonald
1912–34	Arthur Henderson
1935–44	J. S. Middleton
1944–61	Morgan Phillips
1962–8	Len Williams
1968–72	H. R. Nicholas
1973–	Ron Hayward

Bibliography

R. McKenzie, *British Political Parties* (Heinemann 1970).

H. Pelling, *A Short History of the Labour Party* (Macmillan 1972).

G. D. H. Cole, *A Short History of the British Working Class Movement* (Allen & Unwin 1948).

History of the Labour Party from 1914 (Routledge 1969).

J. P. Mackintosh, *The Government and Politics of Britain* (Hutchinson 1971).

D. E. Butler, *The British General Election of 1955* (Cass 1969).

with R. Rose, *The British General Election of 1959* (Cass 1970).

with A. King, *The British General Election of 1964* (Macmillan 1965).

with A. King, *The British General Election of 1966* (Macmillan 1966).

with M. Pinto-Duschinsky, *The British General Election of 1970* (Macmillan 1971).

with D. Stokes, *Political Change in Britain* (Macmillan 1969).

C. R. Attlee, *The Labour Party in Perspective* (Gollancz 1937).

H. Wilson, *The Labour Government, 1964–70* (Weidenfeld/Michael Joseph 1971).

The Relevance of British Socialism (Weidenfeld 1964).

The New Britain (Penguin 1964).

H. Morrison, *Autobiography* (Odhams 1960).

Government and Parliament (Oxford University Press 1964).

George Brown, *In My Way* (Gollancz 1971; Penguin 1972).

H. Dalton, *Memoirs*, three volumes (Muller 1953–9).

F. Williams, *The Life and Times of Ernest Bevin* (Heinemann 1960).

A Prime Minister Remembers (Heinemann 1961).

L. Hunter, *The Road to Brighton Pier* (Barker 1959).

U. Kitzinger, *Diplomacy and Persuasion* (Thames & Hudson 1973).

W. Beckerman (ed.), *The Labour Government's Economic Record* (Duckworth 1972).

Sixteen Fabian Essays (Fabian Society 1972).

P. Jenkins, *The Battle of Downing Street* (Knight 1971).

R. Jenkins, *What Matters Now* (Collins/Fontana 1972).

H. Clegg, *The System of Industrial Relations in Great Britain* (Blackwell 1970).

M. Harrison, *Trade Unions and the Labour Party since 1945* (Allen & Unwin 1960).

V. Allen, *Power in the Trade Unions* (Longmans 1954).

M. Foot, *Aneurin Bevan, 1945-60* (Davis-Poynter 1973).

B. Donoughue and G. W. Jones, *Herbert Morrison* (Weidenfeld and Nicolson 1973).

Trade Union Leadership (Longmans 1957).

Sidney and Beatrice Webb, *History of the Trade Union Movement* (Longmans 1956).

Fabian Society tracts and pamphlets, 11 Dartmouth Street, London SW1.

Annual Reports, Labour Party and TUC.

The Political Quarterly, January-March 1972 and October-December 1972.

This list, indicating some of the sources used in this book, is intended as a guide for further reading only.

For Product Safety Concerns and Information please contact our EU
representative GPSR@taylorandfrancis.com
Taylor & Francis Verlag GmbH, Kaufingerstraße 24, 80331 München, Germany

www.ingramcontent.com/pod-product-compliance
Ingram Content Group UK Ltd.
Pitfield, Milton Keynes, MK11 3LW, UK
UKHW020934180425
457613UK00019B/389